ON TO PERFECTION

Spiritual Maturity

Nate McCollum

ANMC PUBLISHING

ISBN 979-8-9935460-0-1

ACKNOWLEDGEMENTS

First, I want to acknowledge that God has blessed me, protected me, opened up doors for me, prospered me, and filled my life with good things. Next, I acknowledge and thank my wife, Andrea, who has encouraged me to work to complete this book since its conception; and has graciously helped in proofreading the final manuscript. I also acknowledge and give special thanks to several individuals. George Spicer, who helped direct and instruct me in the process of becoming an author. I acknowledge and thank prophets Apostle Sheryl Taylor and Rev. Lisa Bryant, who would every so often encourage me to complete the book God had called me to write. Paul Lee, who like the prophets, would do the same and remind me that God has people that are waiting for my book. Andrew Kardish, my dear friend from high school who is like a brother to me; I thank God that in our frequent conversations, as iron sharpens iron, our conversations helped me to hone and consolidate my thoughts. I also would like to give a special thanks to Rev. D.J. Bryant and Rev. Joseph W. A. Archie III, who graciously agreed to help edit this work. These are all dynamic servants of God who exemplify love and commitment to service. I am honored to be counted as friend to each of you. I also acknowledge and thank God for those special individuals who God has used to plant and water my life, to whom I owe a great deal, especially those who have fulfilled the role of mentor and teacher. I also want to thank and acknowledging everyone that I have not named who has either encouraged me in the writing or been instrumental in making me who I am today. I appreciate your planting and watering in my life.

CONTENTS

INTRODUCTION

Perfection is primarily used to denote that something is without mar or defect. Perfection, in another sense can refer to something that is whole or complete. I have undertaken this work to bring light to several scripture passages that speak of perfection. We should endeavor to try to understand how fallen man, even though he must be redeemed can become perfect. I hold that the Word of God does not require something that He does not enable us to do.

So, to make sense of the command, there are several areas of our lives in which we can be proactive in diminishing the defects and become whole.

Matthew 5:48 Be ye therefore perfect, even as your Father which is in heaven is perfect.

2 Samuel 22:33 God is my strength and power: and he maketh my way perfect.

Ephesians 4:11-12 And he gave some, apostles; and some, prophets; and some, evangelists; and some, pastors and teachers; [12] For the perfecting of the saints, for the work of the ministry, for the edifying of the body of Christ:

Colossians 1:28 Whom we preach, warning every man, and teaching every man in all wisdom; that we may present every man perfect in Christ Jesus:

The overall sense of perfect in these scriptures lean toward a sense of completeness. Throughout this book, think of perfect as the sense of fulfilling lack, removing defect, and becoming whole and complete.

So, let's delve into looking at various aspects of life with the intent to identify and correct those actions and mindsets that could hinder our growth of completeness in our Lord. Hence, let us examine how the Lord can expect imperfect men and women to be perfect.

CHAPTER ONE
CHOSEN

Perfection in any endeavor begins with taking a first step. Any successful professional will tell you that their success began with them taking a first step. More often than not, first steps are like an infant's first steps. That is that they are characterized by a lack of balance. Our first steps can also be characterized somewhat like that. We can experience a sense of unbalance, as we lose the sense of any previous security, as we choose to let go of the old and accept the beginning of all things new. There is another part of our first steps in this new life that remind me of interactions with infants. When my granddaughter was learning to walk, I would be there watching. I was close enough to intervene if she got into trouble but would refrain from blatant intervention that I might not hinder her growth and she would learn to walk. We can rest assured that our first steps are monitored by God, and even though it may look like we will fall, our Father is ever present to lift us up. We have been chosen by God. Be encouraged that although you may feel as if you lack stability and balance in your life, God has chosen and destined you for perfection. We have not chosen him, rather He has chosen us before the foundation of the world.

Our salvation truly rests in the Lord. Our working toward and walking in perfection begins with our acknowledgment, acceptance and realization of who He is. ***Mt. 22:14 For many are called but few are chosen.*** God sent His son to die for the sin of the whole world. The tragedy is that the whole world does not accept the gift that God has freely given. We who know the Lord and love Him would do well to remember that our salvation comes not because of ourselves, but because of the one in whom we believe. The one with whom we have to do is the savior of the world and the deliverer of our soul. The Lord says in ***John 15:16 Ye have not chosen me, but I have chosen you, and ordained you, that ye should go and bring forth fruit....*** Too often we take on a prideful and separatist attitude. It is true that we are a peculiar people, however our peculiarity rests not in our deeds or ourselves, rather it rests in our God and our Lord. Too many of us who take on the label of Christian, take on an attitude of superiority. It wouldn't be so bad if what was realized was the superiority of our God. Unfortunately, too often this is not the case. What is presumed is the superiority of the individual. What makes you better than your unsaved neighbor? Is it your ability to give, or your capacity to care, or the wisdom you possess? Some unsaved philanthropists truly give generously to some chosen cause. Some drunken buddies care and to some degree look out for each other at a level that would put some Christians to shame. To an outsider, the degree in which they share with each other can be staggering. In many cases those with very little resources will share their last with another in desperate need. Don't forget the example of the widow's mite (Mark 12:42). Also in some instances it seems like the world is wiser than some in the church. No, it is not any of the temporal things that make us better. All of these things are outward expressions. ***John 1:12 But as many as received him, to them gave he power to become the sons of God, even to them that believe on his name:***

Many of today's leaders say I will now go and serve the Lord, rather than wait for the Lord to send them. There is a difference between our abilities and our calling. Our abilities can indeed take us quite far, but there is a limit to how far our abilities, (even the ones God blesses us with), can take us. There is no limit to how far our anointing or calling can take us. God imposes the only limits, and that is based on; what He has called us to do, rather than what our abilities enable us to do. The scriptures confirm this when we consider such examples as Moses, Jeremiah, and Gideon (the mighty man of valor who was hiding out). These all complained about their physical limitations. It is further borne out by examples such as David, Paul, and Peter. When they trusted in their own strength, they failed. If we are to surpass the mediocre, and go beyond the impossible and into the miraculous, we must be called, sent, and led by God.

Although this seems like a deep truth, it is actually quite basic. Without God, it is impossible for any of us to be saved.

Isaiah 6:8 Also I heard the voice of the Lord, saying, Whom shall I send, and who will go for us? Then said I, Here am I; send me.

Lots of God's people believe and are erroneously taught that they choose their calling, and which spiritual gifts they will operate in. They believe they can tell God which gifts He should bless them with. We are called to be the members of His body. He is the head. Too often, the body tries to dictate to the head, rather than be submissive to the head. Many go on a mission for God, after having had a glimpse of God, without receiving orders from Him. In warfare, every soldier has orders. His orders tell him when and how to engage the enemy. God is the sovereign one. He is the one who empowers us. Without Him, we have no message and no power. When someone is truly sent, they don't just believe they have been sent. They know they have been sent because they have His voice ringing in their ears and they have His orders in their hands and are led by His Spirit. Consider, even the prophet Isaiah said "here am I Lord, send me". If I can use the analogy, march with the Lord's orders rather than with your own desires. This is not a call for inactivity and slothfulness; rather it is a plea to seek our commander to receive His orders.

Romans 1:6 Among whom are ye also are the called of Jesus Christ. Called to be saints. Just as Jesus called His twelve disciples, He calls today's saints. Just as He called his disciples to be fishers of men, so too has He called us to be fishers of men. We are to catch men for Him, sharing the gospel of Jesus Christ whereby mankind can be saved. Because it is a spiritual work, we cannot do it in our own strength. It is not by power nor by might but by the spirit of the Lord. The apostle Paul shared that in his flesh there was no good thing.

The Spirit decides which gifts He will give to each saint. This is a far cry from what is often propagated today. Men believe that the strength of their calling is that they have chosen the Lord, rather than the blessed truth that He has chosen them. They also believe they choose their calling and gifts. There are some who decide for themselves to become an apostle, evangelist, prophet, pastor or teacher. However, there is a difference between what the Lord has chosen and what men have chosen. Even as we seek him, we seek to walk in the calling that he has chosen for us.

Matthew 7:21-23 Not every one that saith unto me, Lord, Lord, shall enter into the kingdom of heaven; but he that doeth the will of my Father which is in heaven. Many will say to me in that day, Lord, Lord have we not prophesied in thy name? And in thy name have cast out devils? And in thy name done many wonderful works? And then will I profess unto them, I never knew you: depart from me, ye that work iniquity.

There are many people even within the church who are able to perform miraculous works in the name of the Lord Jesus Christ, yet they do not know him. Even Pharoah's magicians mimicked the miracles of Moses. Realize that there are those who love the things of God more than they love the God who blessed them with those things. There are some that enjoy serving God more than they enjoy loving God. I submit that in **Luke 10:38**, Jesus had an encounter with two sisters, Mary and Martha. Martha was encumbered with much serving. However Mary chose the better part, which was to sit at the feet of Jesus and learn of Him. We too have an obligation to learn of Jesus. Once again, I hope I'm not misunderstood as saying I advocate inactivity. What I am saying is that it is far better for us, in our pursuit of perfection, to grow in the grace and knowledge of our Lord and savior Jesus Christ. When it comes to the issue of merely serving him or truly knowing him; I can think of nothing more tragic than to be used by the Lord and not be saved by Him. It is imperative that we learn of Him. It is in the presence of the Lord that we experience fullness of joy. In **Psalm 122**, David expressed his joy at being invited to enter the house of the Lord. I am convinced that he felt that way not because of the edifice but because of the one who dwells between the cherubim within that edifice. This is evidenced by the fact that David maintained a relationship with the Lord even during his time of exile. While he was in exile he could not enter into the temple.

Psalm 27:4 One thing have I desired of the Lord, that will I seek after; that I may dwell in the house of the Lord all the days of my life, to behold the beauty of the Lord, and to inquire in his temple. Within the house of the Lord or the temple were the Holy Place and the Most Holy Place. The ark of the covenant was housed within the Most Holy Place. Within the ark were the articles representing the grace and power of the most powerful God. Over the ark was the Shekinah glory of God, which represented the physical presence of God upon the Earth. David desired to always be in the presence of the Lord.

The love of God is of utmost importance. There are a lot of Christians who want to perform miracles in the name of the Lord, or manifest charismatic gifts; but there are not as many interested in ministering to the Lord. In themselves, religious works are not bad things; but it is better to simply love the Lord. Occasionally I share that I am charismatic (concerning the gifts of the Spirit). However, I am also very careful concerning my charisma. In Christendom, charismatics are those who believe and function in the gifts of the Holy Spirit. This includes such gifts as speaking in tongues, laying on of hands, moving in the power of God, and prophesy (speaking under the unction and representative of God). Secularly, those with charisma are those who by their speech and presence are able to draw and influence people. So, I try to be careful to not misuse my influence. I believe everyone has a sphere of influence. Many people have a degree of authority. However, all authority is delegated. We should be careful to not misuse our authority by improperly using our speech, tone, and deeds. Therefore, I try to be careful, and encourage others to be careful to not use your charisma for self-aggrandizement or the detriment of others.

There are three biblical examples that hint at the impact of influence.

The first example comes from *1 Samuel 3:19-20 And Samuel grew, and the Lord was with him, and did let none of his words fall to the ground. [20] And all Israel from Dan even to Beer-sheba knew that Samuel was established to be a prophet of the Lord.*

let's add some context to these two verses. Samuel was mentored by Eli. Eli was high priest of Israel. Eli had allowed his sons to profane and abuse the office of the priesthood. God gave Samuel a message for Eli that God would remove his house and legacy because of Eli's failure to restrain his sons in the function of their office. Their abuse led the people to despise the priesthood. These men who were supposed to act as intermediaries between God and man were actually causing a rift between the two parties.

The next biblical example is found in *1 Kings 13:18 He said unto him, I am a prophet also as thou art ; and an angel spake unto me by the word of the Lord, saying, Bring him back with thee into thine house, that he may eat bread and drink water. But he lied unto him.*

I have come to understand that using gifts without the balm of love does not bind up wounds, rather it causes division. I realize that my charisma, which is given by God, is not for me to bring glory to myself but to bring glory to the most high God. Nor is it to use against or abuse those for whom Jesus Christ has poured out his life's blood. So, my point is that we have been called by God; and first and foremost we have been called to love God. We have been called to minister the gospel of reconciliation.

The basic tenant of the Jewish faith is based on the Hebrew word " Shema", the first word translated "hear" in *Deuteronomy 6:4 Hear, O Israel: The Lord our God is one Lord: And thou shalt love the Lord thy God with all thine heart, and with all thy soul, and with all thy might.* Jesus elaborates further in *Matthew 22:36-40 Master, which is the great commandment in the law? Jesus said unto him, Thou shalt love the Lord thy God with all thy heart, and with all thy mind. This is the first and great commandment. And the second is like unto it, Thou shalt love thy neighbor as thyself. On these two commandments hang all the law and the prophets.*

When we begin a discussion on perfection, we have to define to some degree what it is that we are to perfect. We begin this discussion with looking at our calling, and answering two questions. First, we must understand whom it is that has called us; then we should know what it is that we have been called to do. The answer to the first question is that God has chosen us and none other than Jesus Christ, the express image of the invisible God has purchased our salvation. Although that sounds like a simple statement, the true importance of that simple statement lies in understanding the identity of just who is this Jesus. I am convinced that one of the main reasons many Christians are stagnated in their growth is because they have not reached a proper understanding of who Jesus is; and therefore have not understood their own identity. They have striven to become great in the world, without putting first the fact that Jesus defines greatness and he does not do it as the world does. Remember how illuminating and liberating it was for Peter when he was able to respond to Jesus' inquiry concerning who men thought he was; with the response that Jesus was the Christ, the Son of the living God. Actually the world's definition of greatness is the opposite of what the Lord calls great.

We have been chosen and called, and that by the sovereign one of the universe. There is none greater than He! The vastness of His greatness is such that when God wanted to give Abraham a promise with surety, He looked upon the Earth and in the heaven; and finding nothing greater than Himself, He had to swear by Himself. So great is this Jesus that when mankind was in need of a savior, He chose to inhabit a body to come down to be our savior. So vast is his greatness, that in regard to salvation, the Revelation account records that John was in weeping because none was found worthy to open the book. As he was watching he saw the lion of the tribe of Judah prevail to open the book; and that lion was the lamb of God.

God is faithful, by whom ye were called unto the fellowship of his Son Jesus Christ our Lord (1 Corinthians 1:9). God is faithful. That is that God is true and He does not lie nor is He deceitful. He does what he says. The word says he does not promise us bread and give us a stone. The meaning of this passage was illuminated to me in the most profound way.

One day as I was in the supermarket, I was walking through an aisle and passed by the bakery section, something in the corner of my eye caught my attention. What I glimpsed caused me to back up and take a closer look. I thought I saw a stone sitting in the bakery case. I remember thinking, this does not make sense. Why would someone put a stone in the bakery case where bread should be? When I took a closer look I found it was not a stone at all. It was a baked loaf of bread. In western society we are used to seeing processed loaves of bread. In Jesus's day, the loaves were baked. In appearance they were similar to stones. The illumination was clear: God does not promise or give things that merely appear to be good. With God, it is more than just appearance. God does not call us for appearance sake. He calls us that we may first be partakers of His marvelous grace, and then become effective ministers of the gospel of reconciliation. The gospel begins, proceeds, and ends with Emmanuel (God with us). For He that began a good work in you is also able to perform it until the day of Jesus Christ. We have been called to set men free, not just in appearance but in reality. In third world countries (also in developed countries), there is often a cry for revolution. Yet, even with that cry is the fear that the deliverer will soon become the oppressor. This is not so with Jesus. He does not exchange one set of shackles for another. Whom the Son has set free is free indeed. We have been called as agents, not to exchange prisoner's shackles but to set men free. The only way we can do that is by introducing them to the great deliverer; the sovereign of creation - Jesus Christ.

I beseech all my brethren as Peter did, that we ought to make our calling and election sure. (1 Peter 1:10). We have been called to be in fellowship with the sovereign of the universe and to bring him praise and glory. Too often we use the gifts the gracious Saviour has blessed us with to bring glory to ourselves. This in turn robs God of his glory. Our calling as prophet, apostle, evangelist, pastor and teacher is merely a means to an end. The means is how we are jointly fitted into his body. The end is that He might be glorified. God have mercy on his people. Too often his people would disobey him, and dishonor those for whom he poured out his precious blood that they receive some personal glory and rob him of His glory. The Lord is crying out that his people would let him be the head of his body. So subtle is the deception of false prophets and false followers, that in Hebrews 4:12 the word of God tells us that the word of God is a divider of soul and spirit. The point is that in ourselves, even in our gifting, we cannot tell the difference. What we often think of as spiritual turns out to be soulish and what is often thought to be soulish is spiritual. It takes the word of God to make the distinction because our ways are not his ways. His thoughts are far above our thoughts. So even in our self-reflection, we have to reflect through the word of God. The word of God speaks to leader and follower alike. God is no respecter of persons because He is over every person. If someone is great, it is because God made him or her to be great. So, even in their greatness, they have to look to the great one - Jesus the Christ. God is a respecter of faith. Faith has one source and one focal point, and that is the person Jesus Christ. We have to be crystal clear on this matter. If we are to grow and go on to perfection, there must be a solid foundation on which we can build. We have been called by the Lord to worship, honor, praise, and glorify the Lord. It does not glorify the Lord to worship Him with our tongue while we are dishonoring Him with our actions. It does us no good to serve Him and not know Him. I can think of no greater tragedy than to be used by the Lord and not be saved by Him. God can and does use anyone. He used Pharaoh. He used a donkey to speak to a prophet, a raven to feed a man, and heathen nations to chastise His people.

God has called us not by our own will but because of God's pleasure. We should keep in mind that our calling is not because of any good thing that we have done. It is solely because of God's love and His good pleasure. There are some that boast on being saved from their childhood. Others boast on their religious experiences, or on their heritage. Our calling is not based on how good we were when we were young. Nor is it based on any of our experiences. Nor is it based on who our parents are. Our calling is based solely on the finished work of Jesus Christ. If we are to go on to perfection, we have to be clear on the foundation.

There is a valuable lesson and a means of great encouragement that we can gain from the experience of the Pharisee Saul as he was converted to become the Apostle Paul. ***Acts 9:13-15 Then Ananias answered, Lord, I have heard by many of this man, how much evil he hath done to thy saints*** *at Jerusalem: [14] And here he hath authority from the chief priests to bind all that call on thy name. [15] But the Lord said unto him, Go thy way: for he is a chosen vessel unto me, to bear my name before the Gentiles, and kings, and the children of Israel.* There may come a time in your walk when people who knew you or are familiar with your reputation before your conversion will refuse to hear or interact with you. This man Ananias responded to almighty God with a reluctance to go to Paul. God had to reaffirm that He had chosen Paul. Paul was a chosen vessel unto God. When the enemies from within and without rise up against you, be comforted with the fact that you are a chosen vessel unto God.

So, to summarize, this book is to either invite you to start or to encourage you along the way of this marvelous journey and to go on to perfection. This journey begins with, is carried out through, and ends with God. *Hebrews 12:2 Looking unto Jesus the author and finisher of our faith.*

CHAPTER TWO

PERFECT YOUR CALLING

MAKE YOUR CALLING SURE

Now that we've reviewed to some degree the importance of the realization that we have been called and chosen by God, it is now time to consider what is it that we've been called to; and what is the nature of that call. First and foremost we have been called to salvation. There are a great number of literary works that are dedicated to defining salvation. This is not a work on soteriology or the doctrine of salvation. However, I do intend to bring some distinction to what it is that we who name the name of Jesus are called to. The first point I want to make is that we have been called to reconciliation. A necessary part of reconciliation is repentance. We have been called to be reconciled to God. That is we have been called to be in right standing before God. In order for that to occur we have to acknowledge our sin and repent. Repentance involves an individual acknowledging their sin, turning from sin and turning to God.

God is awesome, gracious, merciful, and sovereign in His calling and choosing us. This chapter deals with perfecting that calling. However, I have to begin with first posing a question, and then commenting on this: To what were you called? I pose this question because if you do not correctly identify what you were called to, you will attempt to grow and perfect the wrong thing. Some think they have been called to be a Baptist or Methodist or Calvinist or republican or democrat or liberal or conservative; or any such thing. Dear reader, please understand that you have not been called to merely be part of some religious organization, church or ideology. You have been called to be partakers of eternal life through Christ Jesus. Unfortunately, it seems too many are satisfied with a superficial turning of their life. They treat church membership like a club membership. Those new fellowships are viewed as the center of one's life. Jesus, your savior and Lord is the center of life. Unfortunately, that which is meant to lead us and strengthen us in our faith, can subtlety usurp the Lord's position in our life.

An integral facet of this pursuit of perfection involves solidifying or making sure one is truly called. ***2 Peter 1:2-11 Grace and peace be multiplied unto you through the knowledge of God, and of Jesus our Lord, [3] According as his divine power hath given unto us all things that pertain unto life and godliness, through the knowledge of him that hath called us to glory and virtue: [4] Whereby are given*** *unto us exceeding great and precious promises: that by these ye might be partakers of the divine nature, having escaped the corruption that is in the world through lust. [5] And beside this, giving all diligence, add to your faith virtue; and to virtue knowledge; [6] And to knowledge temperance; and to temperance patience; and to patience godliness; [7] And to godliness brotherly kindness; and to brotherly kindness charity. [8] For if these things be in you, and abound, they make you that ye shall neither be barren nor unfruitful in the knowledge of our Lord Jesus Christ. [9] But he that lacketh these things is blind, and cannot see afar off, and hath forgotten that he was purged from his old sins. [10] Wherefore the rather, brethren, give diligence to make your calling and election sure: for if ye do these things, ye shall never fall: [11] For so an entrance shall be ministered unto you abundantly into the everlasting kingdom of our Lord and Saviour Jesus Christ.*

I believe there are a great many people who believe they are called but they lack bearing the fruit which proves their calling. What Peter is advocating is this; if you say you are among the called and elected of God, or even think you belong to that group, you should be about the business of working out your salvation. It is as if Paul was saying if you think you are a part of this group of called out ones, you should be diligent to make sure that what you think is actually true. No one is saved in the vacuum of empty words. The apostle enumerates practical actions which we can diligently engage in to ascertain that we are not merely deceiving or being deceived regarding our calling. We are to first have faith. Some understand "work out your salvation " as work *for* your salvation. Instead it should be understood as working from a place of salvation. Parenthetically, I have come to believe that there are some who say they are Christian but are void of faith. ***Romans 10:13-14 For whosoever shall call upon the name of the Lord shall be saved. [14] How then shall they call on him in whom they have not believed? and how shall they believe in him of whom they have not heard? and how shall they hear without a preacher?*** Consider with me, that when Israel was crying out for salvation, they weren't just seeking salvation for their souls. They were looking forward to salvation from their enemies, their circumstances, and their infirmities. Sometimes I ask myself why is it that we don't ask for or expect deliverance from our physical enemies as Israel once did. They cried for deliverance from Pharaoh and the Egyptians, from the Philistines, from the Hittites and such. The response I come up with is another question. Namely, is it because we just don't call on Him like that, and if not then why not? Is it because we don't really believe in him like that? Lord, help us. I understand that some people believe He exists (even the demons believe and tremble), but have no faith in Him. Jesus Christ is at the center of our calling, as well as the beginning and ending or the alpha and omega. Yet, for some, something else lies at the center of their faith. It could be their own idea of faith or righteousness.

So the first thing we should diligently cultivate is true faith in our savior. As a part of that faith in the Christ we should diligently exercise virtue (moral standards). As we have faith in Christ and live by moral standards, we should diligently increase our knowledge. Someone may argue that they do try to increase their knowledge. Well, here is the rub - is it the knowledge of Jesus Christ? Many increase the knowledge of their party line, but that is not the same thing as the knowledge of God or the Christ. When I was following the rhetoric of the latest political campaign cycle, I noted that even among a segment of the evangelical community, there was a noticeable amount of speech equating American values, personal values, or political values with Christian values. The point I want to make is this, these values may coincide but they are not equal. Rather than merely learn about any of these specific groups, ideas and values; how about actually learning about Jesus? Don't stop there. Be diligent in exercising temperance (self-control). Consider with me, how can one master anything if he can't control himself? Also if one doesn't exhibit self control, how can they be willing or able to submit to God? Add patience to all these things. After doing the will of God we have need of patience. We have to learn to be patient. Patience is often an indicator of faith. When you really believe something, you wait for it. How many of us can recount times when despite the existing circumstance or what others had to say, our response was "just you wait and see". Add godliness. How can one live like the devil when one has been redeemed, converted and become a child of God? Add brotherly kindness. Be diligent about expressing basic human kindness. If you can't express basic kindness, this is not what God has called you to be. Let me share this example the Lord left with us.

Luke 9:52-56 And sent messengers before his face: and they went, and entered into a village of the Samaritans, to make ready for him. [53] And they did not receive him, because his face was as though he would go to Jerusalem. [54] And when his disciples James and John saw this, they said, Lord, wilt thou that we command fire to come down from heaven, and consume them, even as Elias did? [55] But he turned, and rebuked them, and said, Ye know not what manner of spirit ye are of. [56] For the Son of man is not come to destroy men's lives, but to save them . And they went to another village.

The disciples went to a town to prepare for the Lord and the people of the town rejected them. They asked the Lord if they could call down fire from heaven in retaliation for the rejection of those people. Now they thought they were justified because precedent had been set by the prophet Elijah when he called down fire to burn up the messengers of king Ahaziah (**2 Kings 1:10,12,14**). Also there was the incident where Elijah called down fire to burn up the false prophets of Baal along with their sacrifice (**1 Kings 18:37-38**). Jesus rebuked His disciples for invoking Him to call down fire in punishment on the pretense of a misused precedent. Please hear and understand me, if you can't express basic human kindness on the pretense that God wants you to destroy people's lives because they are not for you, you are not representing, nor are your values representative of who God is. He has not come to destroy men's lives but to save them. Finally be diligent in expressing love. Hatred, envy and strife are in some respects the antithesis of what God is. He has come to save and make us whole. Perfection means without imperfection or not being marred. It also means to be complete or whole. This work is mostly dedicated to the journey or us becoming whole which ultimately leads to our perfection, or us being free of any mar or blemish. If you can't love, then you can't be complete. You will be marred by your fear and hatred. Jesus told his disciples, He gave them a new commandment in which they were to love one another. Now, this is striking because love was always a commandment since the institution of the law. As I meditated on what was new about this command, I've come to the conclusion that He wanted them to love but not in a tribal way. That is not to just love your tribe or those people who belong to your group. This is borne out by the message of the Good Samaritan. Jesus was responding to the question of who one should consider as neighbor, since the command was to love one's neighbor. Now I can imagine some asking that question to narrowly define neighbor and would have been shocked and surprised at how broad the obligation was. I can easily imagine such a thing because it is easy to see this is what exists in our present day culture. Unfortunately such tribal thinking even exists within evangelical circles.

In some ways our election is like a two sided coin. On the one side is the fact that we've been chosen by God, as we have elaborated on in chapter one. On the other side is the truth that we work out our salvation. This truth is important because there are some who lay claim to salvation because they join a particular church. They believe that because they put their name on the church role, it grants them certain privileges. I've said to church members, "This ain't no country club."

That is you can't come into the church with the attitude that you join the club, pay your dues and are afforded all the rights and privileges of membership. The purpose of joining with the church or the "ekklesia" is to be counted among the "called out ones" and to grow in the knowledge of Christ and to encourage each other in Christ.

I know that sometimes I may sound very critical and to some it may seem that I am against the church. This is not true. What I am against is the false sense of security that some may adopt, when they adhere to a religious system void of intimacy with the living God. How many people do you know that live contrary to the will and word of God on Saturday night and believe that all they have to do is show up at church on Sunday to make amends? Or how about people that don't love their neighbors and think they're OK because they partook of communion? Or what of those who deliberately, consistently, and blatantly sin; yet feel that they are covered because they pay their tithes? My friends, these are all things that good church folks can do.

However, the apostle Paul said that he travailed for the saints at Galatia until Christ was to be formed in them.

Luke 3:7-8 Then said he to the multitude that came forth to be baptized of him, O generation of vipers, who hath warned you to flee from the wrath to come? [8] Bring forth therefore fruits worthy of repentance, and begin not to say within yourselves, We have Abraham to our father: for I say unto you, That God is able of these stones to raise up children unto Abraham. To make your calling and election sure, you have to live like someone who has been redeemed from their old life and live a new life dependent on God's grace. ***Romans 1:16 For I am not ashamed of the gospel of Christ: for it is the power of God unto salvation to every one that believeth; to the Jew first, and also to the Greek.*** Actually, we are called to salvation. It is not affiliations with groups or organizations to which we are called. Rather it is salvation or reconciliation to which we have been called; and we have been given the ministry of reconciliation. We are reconciled to God and called to preach and work toward the reconciliation of others; that they might be reconciled to God and each other. We must stop warring with God and come into a right relationship with Him. We have been called to love God and to serve, worship, and love Him in the bond of an eternal holy relationship.

What was happening in this passage was that John saw all these people coming to be baptized. He realized many of them had heard or realized that there would be a day of wrath or judgment to come, and they were seeking to be baptized as a sort of insurance policy to escape the coming judgment of God. Incidentally, at different times in history the attitude was different concerning when to be baptized. At one point the mindset was to be baptized as soon as possible so your future sins would be covered. At another time the idea was to wait until the last possible moment so that all of the sins you had committed would be covered. Both views can give a subtle license to sin. John was against all this. He said, in essence, you can only escape the day of wrath by living a godly life, and you can only live a godly life by truly turning to the Lord. So, are you sure of your calling and election? Are you sure you are saved?

Make sure your calling is true by truly living for the Lord. Don't take on a "country club" mindset. Don't develop a false sense of security. Rather, join the ekklesia, fellowship with the saints. Mutually uplift one another, and grow in the knowledge and grace of our Lord and savior Jesus Christ. ***1 Corinthians 10:12 Wherefore let him that thinketh he standeth take heed lest he fall.*** Paul, makes the case as he draws from examples in Israel's history that we must actually take heed to the word of God and stand. It is not enough just to have spiritual experiences. ***1 Corinthians 10:1-5 Moreover, brethren, I would not that ye should be ignorant, how that all our fathers were under the cloud, and all passed through the sea; [2] And were all baptized unto Moses in the cloud and in the sea; [3] And did all eat the same spiritual meat; [4] And did all drink the same spiritual drink:***

for they drank of that spiritual Rock that followed them: and that Rock was Christ. [5] But with many of them God was not well pleased: for they were overthrown in the wilderness. You see, many people depend on their spiritual experiences. This is true even for people today. However, it was not enough for Israel, nor is it enough for believers today. Our experience must actually be mixed with faith in God. It is when we take heed and actually live by the word that we are actually demonstrating faith in God. Is your calling and election sure? I would dare to say that if you want to stand or merely think you stand, you must take heed to the word of God. Now, let me explain what it means to take heed. Taking heed involves several steps. First you have to hear the instructions. In the physical biological sense, hearing involves sound entering the ear gate. That can fail to happen. Once, when I was young; as my brother was sitting in front of the television, I was calling him. He did not hear me. Although I was just a few feet away from him, he failed to hear me. I got a little worried because I began to yell louder and louder and it still took him a while to hear me. Maybe you can relate to this example. Perhaps you spoke to a child or someone to give them instructions. Only to find that you had to ask them if they heard what you said. Also, in the present there are times when I'm distracted that I don't hear what is being said to me. My wife would attest to the fact that there are times when I don't hear her because my mind is elsewhere. So, your mind can't be elsewhere if you are going to hear the Lord's instruction. Second, you have to receive or understand what was said. A good tool of communication is to repeat back your understanding of what was said. I've had to employ this tool as both presenter and receiver. As presenter, I have had to tell my grandson to repeat what I just told him. As receiver, I've said to my wife "what I understand you saying is...." I can't enumerate the number of times communication has failed because of misunderstanding. I've come to believe that good successful communication is in itself a sort of miracle. This is partly because people have so many filters that effect their reception of any type of communication. So, it would be helpful to accept what is said without subjecting it to our filters. The good thing is that God is a God of miracles. The third and final step of heeding is to actually follow through and carry out the instruction. In the example of instructing a child, they can hear what was said to them and understand what was said, but if they don't follow through and carry out the instruction; they have not heeded. So, dear reader if you would have any inkling of standing in an assurance of calling and election; I encourage you to do these three things; hear, understand and obey. If you fail to hear what the Spirit of the Lord is saying, or fail to understand, or follow through with obedience, how can you have any faith in your stand?

Now, someone out there will respond by blaming God for them not hearing Him. What language do you think God speaks? God is the creator of language. He was the instigator in confounding the language of men. Also, through the Holy Spirit (the third person in the Godhead), He caused men of different languages, nations and creeds to hear the good news of God in their own language. All of this is to say that God is able to speak to you so that you can understand.

Romans 10:13-18 For whosoever shall call upon the name of the Lord shall be saved. [14] How then shall they call on him in whom they have not believed? and how shall they believe in him of whom they have not heard? and how shall they hear without a preacher? [15] And how shall they preach, except they be sent? as it is written, How beautiful are the feet of them that preach the gospel of peace, and bring glad tidings of good things! [16] But they have not all obeyed the gospel. For Esaias saith, Lord, who hath believed our report? [17] So then faith cometh by hearing, and hearing by the word of God. [18] But I say, Have they not heard? Yes verily, their sound went into all the earth, and their words unto the ends of the world.

You cannot blame God for your failure to hear His word. The blame can only be attributed to an unwillingness to hear.

Matthew 7:24-25 Therefore whosoever heareth these sayings of mine, and doeth them, I will liken him unto a wise man, which built his house upon a rock: [25] And the rain descended, and the floods came, and the winds blew, and beat upon that house; and it fell not: for it was founded upon a rock.

You cannot blame God for your failure to perform His sayings. The blame can only be attributed to rebellion.

Galatians 6:7-8,18 Be not deceived; God is not mocked: for whatsoever a man soweth, that shall he also reap. [8] For he that soweth to his flesh shall of the flesh reap corruption; but he that soweth to the Spirit shall of the Spirit reap life everlasting. [18] Brethren, the grace of our Lord Jesus Christ be with your spirit. Amen.

For many years, whenever I read, thought about, or shared this passage; I always thought of it as a dire warning to those who were only interested in satisfying their fleshly desires. Somehow, even though I now clearly see one main point with two different streams diverging from that single point; in the past I only saw one thing. The one thing I saw was if you feed your fleshy desires you will die. I now see that the main point is that God promises everlasting life to those who choose him. The two streams are a choice between life and death with the caveat being that self-deception is possible. One can believe they are saved and will receive the promises of God while truly only being concerned with their own desires. Realize however that our desires can consist of "good" works and still be done selfishly. I'm sure the disciples would have considered it a good thing when they wanted to call down fire from heaven on those who rejected their heralding Jesus. The good news is that this passage is not just about the reward of the wicked. It is first and foremost about the ever lasting life God promises to those who would sow to their spirit. You see, don't deceive yourself into thinking that you will receive anything but corruption (and ultimately corruption reaps death) if you continue to walk in the flesh.

Conversely, neither should you allow the enemy of your soul to deceive you into believing you shall receive anything other than everlasting life as a reward from God. Make your calling sure by seeking spiritual things; to be more precise, seek God in the face of Jesus Christ. So, is your salvation sure?

The following is a good passage to use to sum up this section as we consider what we are called to and in essence to give some sense of purpose

2 Corinthians 5:17-21 Therefore if any man be in Christ, he is a new creature: old things are passed away; behold, all things are become new. [18] And all things are of God, who hath reconciled us to himself by Jesus Christ, and hath given to us the ministry of reconciliation; [19] To wit, that God was in Christ, reconciling the world unto himself, not imputing their trespasses unto them; and hath committed unto us the word of reconciliation. [20] Now then we are ambassadors for Christ, as though God did beseech you by us: we pray you in Christ's stead, be ye reconciled to God. [21] For he hath made him to be sin for us, who knew no sin; that we might be made the righteousness of God in him.

We have not been called to endless causes, although a good cause may indeed be part of our true calling. We have been called to be reconciled to God by Jesus Christ. I believe the bulk of instruction in the Bible is to tell us how we are both passively and proactively reconciled. That is realizing what is done on our behalf as well as what we do. So, be reconciled to God

I have two points to make in conclusion of this chapter. One in the negative and one in the positive. First, do not be taken in by the deception of falsely believing you are saved and pleasing God if you are not. Do *not* follow the example of those who thought they were pleasing God when they actually were far from Him. We discussed some of these examples. There are examples like Saul before his conversion to Paul. The example of the disciples invoking Jesus to allow them to call down fire from heaven, and lastly the example of the seven churches of Asia Minor in the book of Revelation.

Second, do earnestly seek the Lord.

CHAPTER THREE

PERFECT YOUR FOCUS

SINGLENESS OF MIND

Matthew 6:22 The light of the body is the eye: if therefore thine eye be single thy whole body shall be full of light. The eye, which is the organ by which we see, must be single. That is, it cannot be divided. It cannot have its focus on two different things. Similarly, in society, those who are on the pinnacle of success are there because they had a singular focus. They spent their time, energy, and resources to become proficient in their chosen endeavor. We too become proficient in walking in the grace in which we stand as we hold on to a single purpose. We have need of many things during our sojourn here in life. However, we must learn to distinguish between needs and desires. From there we learn to prioritize, and our priority must be to put God first. Therefore, our true need is one thing, and that one thing is to lay hold of the finished work of Jesus Christ.

Let me put it this way; it is a necessity for each of us to partake of food and water. *__Matthew 4:4 But he answered and said, It is written, Man shall not live by bread alone, but by every word that proceedeth out of the mouth of God.__* Without these substances, we would perish. Yet, we have in *__Job 23:12 …I have esteemed the words of his mouth more than my necessary food.__* Job felt that the single most important thing necessary for life was the words that God had for him. You see, without the word of God we would perish. The Lord speaks life into our lives. Just as He spoke into the darkness "let there be light" and there was light, so He speaks life into our lives. See the light! Jesus is indeed the light of the world and His light brings life.

Take into consideration that the moon is not the primary source of light, yet we have moonlight. My point is this, although light might proceed from us, as we allow our light to shine; like the moon, we are not the great source of light. The moon is the lesser light and the sun is the greater light. Jesus is the light of the world. So great is His light, that He outshines the light from both the moon and the sun. *__Revelation 21:23 And the city had no need of the sun, neither of the moon, to shine in it: for the glory of God did lighten it, and the lamb is the light thereof.__* Jesus is the only source of light.

We can all become concerned and encumbered with many things, but we must keep our eyes on Jesus. The distractions, which come to move our focus, are subtle. They are the cares of the world. It is of the utmost importance to stay in a right standing with God, and not to become encumbered with the things of the world, including our own works of righteousness. The only way to do this is through a humble submission to God. If we don't spend adequate time with our Lord, we can easily lose our focus and look more at the work than we look toward the Lord. It is all a matter of focus. Physiologically, when we focus on something, we adjust our vision so that we might see something near rather than far, or far rather than near. There are those who are near sighted or farsighted. They can only clearly see what's in their respective range. They need some type of corrective lens to focus outside of their range. In a sense, we all have vision that is deficient in some way. We need the word of God to correct our focus. ***Psalm 119:105 Thy word is a lamp unto my feet, and a light unto my path.*** Similarly, our singleness of mind should be such that we see Jesus, over and above our work. After all, He is the one to be exalted and lifted up.

Our mindset can take us a long way. Are you a pessimist, an optimist, or something in between? Do you focus on the good or the bad? Is there anything that drives you, or strengthens you, or encourages you, or hinders you? Is there anything you can focus on that keeps you grounded? In this chaotic world, when the storms of life blow while we juggle many cares, it can become difficult to not be overwhelmed.

Luke 10:41-42 And Jesus answered and said unto her, Martha, Martha, thou art careful and troubled about many things: [42] But one thing is needful: and Mary hath chosen that good part, which shall not be taken away from her.

Martha was doing a good thing. She was busy with serving. We too can be busy with doing good things; fulfilling obligations, providing for needs of family and loved ones, providing emotional support where necessary, and overall doing things that a caring responsible person would undertake. However, while we try to fulfill these different roles, we can become burdened as the worry and anxiety of our attempt overtakes us. Like Martha, we can become careful and troubled about many things.

Luke 10:39 And she had a sister called Mary, which also sat at Jesus' feet, and heard his word.

Mary chose the better part because she chose not to neglect to sit at Jesus' feet. I want to make sure that you don't take this as an example to not do things we should do in service to others. This is not to dismiss the value of such things. Rather, this is to look to Jesus and to not carry the burdens and worries in one's own strength. I can see fathers and mothers, sons and daughters, husbands and wives, workers and bosses, teachers and students, and mentors and mentees; all being concerned and worried about performance and outcomes. I'm not dismissing any of the importance of your service. However, like the Lord's response to Martha, I believe there is a better way. We can metaphorically sit at the feet of Jesus. We can learn of Him and from Him. We can hear His words. We can draw strength from Him. All of the work has a purpose. As we sit at His feet and draw from Him, the work and therefore the worry does not overshadow the purpose. It's not only purpose that can be overshadowed by the drive to perform; being lost in the valley of decision can also be attributed to a loss of focus.

Matthew 6:23 But if thine eye be evil, thy whole body shall be full of darkness. If therefore the light that is in thee be darkness, how great is that darkness!

I remember one day, a friend of mine, walked into the office and was really excited about his ability to see clearly with his new eyeglasses. In my confusion, I asked why he was so excited. He had worn glasses, as long as I had known him. His response to clear up my confusion was to share that he had gotten so used to his impaired vision that he didn't realize he wasn't seeing clearly until his vision was corrected with new glasses. There is a myriad of causes that can lead to a lack of focus. This passage has some correlation with some of the physiological and spiritual problems concerning the function of the eye. When the scripture refers to an evil eye, it's talking about a diseased eye. There are several eye diseases that lead to a loss of or compromise of focus. Let us examine some common eye disorders with the intent to glean understanding of the scriptural passage, biological function of the eye, and spiritual application of certain truths. The light of the body is the eye. The eye is the organ through which we receive light and then that light is converted somehow into information. The eye can be single and healthy, or it can be evil and diseased. If the eye is healthy, then health spreads throughout the body. If the eye is diseased, the entire body suffers from that lack of focus. Some of you might remember the lyrics "I can see clearly now....". The surprising thing is that like my buddy who walked in my office that day; many people see dimly and don't realize their vision is out of focus because they have become used to seeing things that way. Consider these eye problems. Cataracts are categorized by a clouding of the lens. In your spiritual walk, sometimes your vision can be clouded by something else and you can be unaware of your diminished vision because you have become accustomed to seeing through a faulty lens. Glaucoma is characterized by nerve damage often caused by elevated fluid pressure in the eyes. So too, can a build up of pressure cause our focus to be lost due to the damage caused by the build up. It is imperative that if we want to continue to see clearly, we must cast our cares upon Him and not carry those heavy burdens alone. ***Matthew 11:28-29 Come unto me, all ye that labour and are heavy laden, and I will give you rest. [29] Take my yoke upon you, and learn of me; for I am meek and lowly in heart: and ye shall find rest unto your souls.***

Then there are those who suffer from either near sightedness or far sightedness. These two conditions can be treated with corrective lenses. Spiritually, there are those who can only see things close to them or alternately see only those things with which they have nothing to do with. Like eye glass wearers, some believers have to correct their vision so that they can see clearly. When it comes to the issue of focus, not only is clarity of focus important but singleness of focus is equally important.

Learn to perfect your focus. Jettison those things which prevent you from seeing God clearly. For some that means renouncing some of the things you've been doing, walking away from some of your relationships, no longer going to some of the places you frequent, tearing down your old ramparts, and burning old bridges. All these hindrances can cloud your focus; preventing you from seeing clearly. You can't serve two masters. For some, the reason why their vision is unfocused is because they have too many masters. They have too many points of focus. Multitasking is fine except for when the tasks are diametrically opposed in purpose. Perfect your focus. Tune in to one master, one Lord, one purpose. For those who are still searching to identify and understand their purpose, I offer these suggestions to pursue. How about laying hold of eternal life and serving God in the beauty of holiness? Or escaping the curse of sin and death? Or partaking of and enjoying the benevolence of the almighty God?

We can choose to live either spiritually minded or carnally minded. We can have a temporal mindset or an eternal mindset. When our mindset is temporal, we live in the temporary - the now. When we have an eternal mindset, we live for eternity. Living for eternity does not mean that you neglect living in the present. However, it does take into consideration that your present reflects upon and in some ways determine your eternity.

There are many decisions to be made. There are many forks in the road where we must choose which path to take. There are times we make choices based on what we think is correct, right, orthodox, or acceptable. Often, there are too many factors involved in the choices. Factors which include such things as considering what others might think, the effect on one's career or standing, or the profit one could receive. Many factors can cloud one's reasoning. When this cloud appears in the valley of decision, it's best to settle one's self, and focus on choosing that which pleases God.

This chapter is all about how we see things and what we focus on. We should see Jesus and focus on Him.

Psalm 34:5 They looked unto him, and were lightened: and their faces were not ashamed. We can choose to look at our problems and struggles or we can choose to look to Him.

If we are to grow toward maturity, we have to put our focus on the Lord.

Philippians 4:8 Finally, brethren, whatsoever things are true, whatsoever things are honest, whatsoever things are just, whatsoever things are pure, whatsoever things are lovely, whatsoever things are of good report; if there be any virtue, and if there be any praise, think on these things.

Practice looking for the good. Practice expecting God to deliver you, bless you, and cause His face to shine upon you.

Practice endeavoring to please God. Be intentional in choosing to look to God in order to please Him.

Matthew 5:14-16 Ye are the light of the world. A city that is set on an hill cannot be hid. [15] Neither do men light a candle, and put it under a bushel, but on a candlestick; and it giveth light unto all that are in the house. [16] Let your light so shine before men, that they may see your good works, and glorify your Father which is in heaven.

We have been called to be emissaries of the word of God. We *can* all become concerned and encumbered with many things, but we must keep our eye on Jesus. The distractions which come to move our focus are very subtle. They are the cares of this world. It is of the utmost importance to stay in a right standing with God, and not to become burdened with the things of the world, which may include our own religious works. The only way to do this is through a humble submission to God. Unless we spend adequate time with our Lord, we can lose our focus by looking more at the work than we look toward the Lord. It is all a matter of focus.

Parenthetically, let me mention the following concerning the word of God. Since the word of God has the role of directing us, we must earnestly heed the word of God. We cannot rely on our own feelings or intuition. We can not rely on our understanding, no matter how sanctified we believe our understanding to be. His thoughts are far above our thoughts.

Over time, as I preached and heard others preach, I realized that among the preachers everyone was not saying the same thing, even though many were using the same scriptures. Different people understood the scriptures differently and some were misinterpreting the word of God. I believe a major factor to misinterpreting scriptures is that people often try to find a scripture to support their point of view instead of letting the scriptures form their point of view. Some excuse their arrogance by claiming they have the spirit of God. We ought to question as to whether the things we receive actually come from God because they could come from one of three sources: God, the devil, or self. The truth is we know the spirit of God by the word of God. We can not go on to perfection, even in the matter of walking in the power of His spirit, unless we are willing to go outside of ourselves and be directed by the word of God.

Isaiah 26:3 Thou wilt keep him in perfect peace, whose mind is stayed on thee: because he trusteth in thee. The Lord keeps us in perfect peace and because the quality of such peace is perfect, it surpasses our understanding. We maintain that standing as long as we keep our mind or focus on the Lord. This is demonstrated by the biblical account of Peter sinking while walking on the water after taking his eyes off of Jesus. If the truth were told, we would testify that it is not just the world that does not understand. We do not quite understand ourselves how we can have peace in certain situations. God, however, is glorified, because we as well as the world, know that this is not a natural peace; and we give glory to God as the source of our peace. As the storm clears, it can be a great testimony to the grace and sovereignty of God. Notice the subtlety of this, we keep our mind focused on Him; not the work, our troubles, or our gifts; only on Him. To focus unduly on our gifts, is a false focus. To focus on anything other than the Lord, although it may come from the Lord is a false focus. We cannot focus more on what the Lord gave us to do than we do on the Lord himself. Israel boasted of their privileged position, rather than focus on the Lord. The result was that the Lord used the heathen to chastise his people because of their sin and idolatry. It is no different today in that there are those whose boast is in how the Lord has gifted them. Our boasting however should be in the Lord, not in our status. We have to maintain our focus. It is by grace that we have been saved through faith, and that is not of ourselves, it is the gift of God. There was a point in time as recorded in the scriptures that the seventy disciples that the Lord had sent out returned to him, boasting in the fact that the demons were subject to them. He chided them they should not boast in the fact that the demons were subject to them, rather they should glory in the fact that their names were written in the book of life. They had begun to lose their focus. Their focus was on what they had done rather than what Jesus had accomplished and secured for them (Luke 10:20).

I know there are times we can feel trepidation when the Lord points us in a direction which is uncomfortable or one in which the outcome may seem bleak to us. It is at times like these when we really can't afford to lose our focus. To do so causes us undue fear and anxiety. We don't have to worry about the outcome of an act or decision when the source of our choice of direction is from the Lord. He knows how to deliver the godly, and He does not give us a stone when He promises bread.

Isaiah 6:1 In the year that king Uzziah died I saw also the Lord sitting upon a throne, high and lifted up, and his train filled the temple. The prophet is recounting his experience of coming to an awareness of the Lord. It is striking to me that this awareness came at a time around the death of king Uzziah. Though Uzziah was one of the good kings of Israel, he wound up essentially dying in quarantine. I don't know if in the wake of king Uzziah's death, Isaiah was considering his benevolent life or his ignoble death. I do know that at this point Isaiah saw the Lord. The point of application I want to draw from this example is that at some point Isaiah stopped looking at the king and started looking at The Lord. When someone is noble we can look at them as an example but we truly have to look beyond them and look toward their source. If someone is ignoble we can see their outcome and choose not to follow their course. In either case we have to look beyond people in order to see the Lord. I fear that even now some of my readers have not yet seen the Lord. This in part is because their focus has been on some person.

It is not just persons that can be the object of our focus. Equally our focus can be on a particular ideology. That ideology can supplant the importance of the word of God. If you become more concerned with church protocol than Jesus, your focus needs to be adjusted. If you are more concerned with the doctrines of men than the principles of God, your focus has to be adjusted. If your five points or six steps, or whatever enumeration you devise takes prominence over the simplicity of Christ, you have lost your focus. My wife preached a sermon some years ago, "It's not about you, it's all about Him." When it becomes all about you, whether it be your hardships or glory, you have lost focus and need to readjust. Be careful when your ideological precepts become more important than the word of God and the work and person of Jesus Christ.

CHAPTER FOUR

PERFECT YOUR IDENTITY

Many people build their identity on what they do. Their identity is inextricably intwined with what they do. They equate their profession with their identity. This can also be true with their perception of how others view them. There are people who after spending years in a career, feel a great loss when that career ends. Unfortunately, some of that feeling of loss is because their identity was completely built and defined by their career.

Years ago, a friend of mine gave me something to consider. He asked me to ponder how difficult it might be for someone to be a great salesman and a great Christian. At first, I didn't understand how those two things could be at odds with one another. He elaborated. The salesman's motto is, do anything to close the deal. The Christian motto ought to be, do everything to please the Lord. So what happens when those two purposes conflict?

Now, to be clear, this is not to pick on a particular profession. It is not about the profession at all. This is not to call out in condemnation any profession, career, societal standing or hobby. What is at issue is that people self identify by what they do rather than who they are; and who they are is not merely defined by their occupation. It is important to rehearse who you are to reach completeness and wholeness. Here are a few passages to help.

Psalm 139:14 I will praise thee; for I am fearfully and wonderfully made: marvellous are thy works; and that my soul knoweth right well.

Galatians 2:20 I am crucified with Christ: nevertheless I live; yet not I, but Christ liveth in me: and the life which I now live in the flesh I live by the faith of the Son of God, who loved me, and gave himself for me.

Psalm 1:1-2 Blessed is the man that walketh not in the counsel of the ungodly, nor standeth in the way of sinners, nor sitteth in the seat of the scornful. [2] But his delight is in the law of the Lord ; and in his law doth he meditate day and night.

Psalm 84:5 Blessed is the man whose strength is in thee; in whose heart are the ways of them.

Psalm 84:12 O Lord of hosts, blessed is the man that trusteth in thee.

Psalm 115:13-15 He will bless them that fear the Lord, both small and great. [14] The Lord shall increase you more and more, you and your children. [15] Ye are blessed of the Lord which made heaven and earth.

Psalm 128:1 Blessed is every one that feareth the Lord ; that walketh in his ways.

Psalm 91:2-3 I will say of the Lord, He is my refuge and my fortress: my God; in him will I trust. [3] Surely he shall deliver thee from the snare of the fowler, and from the noisome pestilence.

I hope you self identify as a Christian. What does it mean to be a Christian?

The -ian suffix refers to an adherent or follower. So I want to encourage and challenge that we wholly complete our adherence to Christ. My daughter is an ardent Philadelphia Eagles fan. During football season, she is always loud and full of energy. Don't dare to demean her team or promote another. Some of you can relate and you understand because you have a favorite team, actor, author or group.

Some people are Christians but don't wholly follow the Lord. Years ago, my wife and I used to watch Naruto, an anime cartoon. After several seasons she lost interest. She would say she was a Naruto fan. I would respond saying she wasn't a true Naruto fan. She stopped being an adherent Naruto follower. If you've repented of your sins and name the name of Christ, it is not up to anyone else to say who is and who isn't a follower. However, I can encourage others to more fully become a follower. Understand that there are lukewarm and carnal Christians. The scriptures declare that God would rather we be hot or cold, not lukewarm.

One thing people tend to do is label people based on their own perceptions of what that individual does. Their condemnation may sound something like this: "You are not a real man", or "you are not a real Christian." Their condemnation is based on what they think that person should be doing according to their point of view. In light of this, I recommend the following: try to refrain from forcing an identity on someone else or receive your identity from someone else. Instead, receive your identity from the Lord. Let the Lord give you your identity. For we bear the imago Dei, the image of God. Because we are created in the image of God; the more successfully we are able to reflect that image, the more secure we become in our sense of identity and struggle less with understanding who we are. ***Matthew 11:29 Take my yoke upon you, and learn of me; for I am meek and lowly in heart: and ye shall find rest unto your souls.***

Prior to my lung transplant, I had to walk around with an oxygen cylinder. I remember one time I was preaching with that oxygen tank with a nasal cannula in my nose. On that pulpit, in the middle of my sermon, I felt a sense of pity from someone. I didn't know the source. I just felt the need to address and teach by my example. So, I shared these words. "I hope you don't just see an old preacher on oxygen. I hope you understand that you are seeing someone who is kept and sustained by the power of God." I understood that I was not defined by my disabilities or limitations. My identity is I am a child of God. I am sustained, provided for, and protected by God.

I once heard someone ask of his detractors, why they thought the power of the devil to take him was greater than the power of God to keep him. ***Romans 8:33-35 Who shall lay any thing to the charge of God's elect? It is God that justifieth. [34] Who is he that condemneth? It is Christ that died, yea rather, that is risen again, who is even at the right hand of God, who also maketh intercession for us. [35] Who shall separate us from the love of Christ? shall tribulation, or distress, or persecution, or famine, or nakedness, or peril, or sword?***

Self identify as someone kept by the power of God. Someone who cannot be overtaken by any force; physical or spiritual. Now understand that does not mean you won't be affected by events and circumstances. It only means that ultimately, when you are a child of God, redeemed by the blood of Christ Jesus, that identity keeps you secure in Him. He is our salvation.

John 1:12 But as many as received him, to them gave he power to become the sons of God, even to them that believe on his name:

Sometimes in order to stand and overcome you have to affirm who you are.

Psalm 20:7 Some trust in chariots, and some in horses: but we will remember the name of the Lord our God.

The greatest thing about who you are is the connection with who He is.

Acts 17:28 For in him we live, and move, and have our being; as certain also of your own poets have said, For we are also his offspring.

Hebrews 1:3 Who being the brightness of his glory, and the express image of his person, and upholding all things by the word of his power, when he had by himself purged our sins, sat down on the right hand of the Majesty on high;

Every person has an inherent worth. Your worth is not earned. It is a given. You have worth, not because of what you do, but because of who you are. You are created by God. When you believe in and receive Him, you have been translated into the kingdom of God.

Psalm 139:14 I will praise thee; for I am fearfully and wonderfully made: marvellous are thy works; and that my soul knoweth right well.

This might come as a surprise, but there are some ministers who are more caught up in what they do than who they are. They don't relish in the blessing of who they are apart from what they do. Their whole identity is derived from their position, title or job.

Luke 10:17-20 And the seventy returned again with joy, saying, Lord, even the devils are subject unto us through thy name. [18] And he said unto them, I beheld Satan as lightning fall from heaven. [19] Behold, I give unto you power to tread on serpents and scorpions, and over all the power of the enemy: and nothing shall by any

means hurt you. [20] Notwithstanding in this rejoice not, that the spirits are subject unto you; but rather rejoice, because your names are written in heaven.

The disciples being addressed here were rejoicing in their power. Jesus wanted them to rejoice in their identity. The problem with ministers not rejoicing in their inherent worth is the same as in the secular. What happens when the job or assignment ends? What about when your assignment does not measure up to someone else's assignment? Does that mean you are worth less than someone else? Or if you have more, does that make you more important and valuable?

Luke 12:6-7 Are not five sparrows sold for two farthings, and not one of them is forgotten before God? [7] But even the very hairs of your head are all numbered. Fear not therefore: ye are of more value than many sparrows.

There is no connection to status, position or spiritual authority with the inherent worth God gives people. It is unfortunate that some people make such connections. Some try to over perform to earn blessings from the Lord.

Ephesians 1:3 Blessed be the God and Father of our Lord Jesus Christ, who hath blessed us with all spiritual blessings in heavenly places in Christ:

We don't work for blessing. We work from a position of already being blessed. You may be someone who finds you are stuck in a performance carousel seeking worth, approval, and acceptance. Or you may be someone, who because of a change in role, find yourself questioning your worth and purpose. I want to encourage you and reiterate that your identity is in God and your worth comes from Him. He does not determine worth based on position, wealth, title or any such thing. He loves the world and invites us to receive and respond to His love. So, strive to take your identity from your relationship with the Lord; above, beyond, and apart from how you work out your salvation. It's not what you do that determines who you are; rather, who you are influences what you do.

CHAPTER FIVE
PERFECT YOUR FAITH

For some faith amounts to a leap off of a cliff into the dark abyss. I do not believe in such blind faith. I do not believe the scriptures endorse jumping wildly into the unknown. We don't run headlong into death and destruction. That is how some run to their ruin. Rather, we jump readily into the known. Not the known in every minute detail, but the knowing of following God. We seek God so that He can reveal, lead, and direct.

So we don't plunge into the unknown. We earnestly follow where God leads. Blind faith leads to scenarios like the Jim Jones cult, or the Branch Davidian fiasco or any incident where individuals blindly march to their demise. True faith proceeds not from the unknown, rather from knowing God. Faith from knowing that God is fully able to perform what He says. There is no failure in Him. Don't take a leap into the unknown rather confidently follow after a reliable, trustworthy and faithful God.

Matthew 4:5-7 Then the devil taketh him up into the holy city, and setteth him on a pinnacle of the temple, [6] And saith unto him, If thou be the Son of God, cast thyself down: for it is written, He shall give his angels charge concerning thee: and in their hands they shall bear thee up, lest at any time thou dash thy foot against a stone. [7] Jesus said unto him, It is written again, Thou shalt not tempt the Lord thy God.

Take care. The dare to cast yourself into destruction can be more akin to the voice of the deceiver and the tempter enticing you to tempt God; than a legitimate act of faith.

Hebrews 11:6 But without faith it is impossible to please him: for he that cometh to God must believe that he is, and that he is a rewarder of them that diligently seek him.

Some find it difficult to mature their faith because they have not truly settled within themselves that God is, and He rewards. They expect evil and not good from the Lord. Perhaps they see God as a disciplinarian but not as the lover of their soul. Or they see Him like a permissive lover who does not demand justice or righteousness.

James 1:7-8 For let not that man think that he shall receive any thing of the Lord. [8] A double minded man is unstable in all his ways.

The double mindedness is not just going back and forth on what color to wear or any number of choices one might make. No. The double minded man is the one who waivers on who God is, specifically, His sovereignty. He is one who is prone to change his mind, or waiver on having a conviction that God rewards and does not harm those who diligently seek after Him.

1 Corinthians 10:1-5 Moreover, brethren, I would not that ye should be ignorant, how that all our fathers were under the cloud, and all passed through the sea; [2] And were all baptized unto Moses in the cloud and in the sea; [3] And did all eat the same spiritual meat; [4] And did all drink the same spiritual drink: for they drank of that spiritual Rock that followed them: and that Rock was Christ. [5] But with many of them God was not well pleased: for they were overthrown in the wilderness.

Sometimes, to help understand what something is, it is also helpful to understand what it is not. All of Israel shared the same spiritual experience that Moses had. They were all delivered from Egypt by God's mighty hand. They all crossed the Red Sea on dry land. They were all led by a cloud during the day and a pillar of fire at night to guide them on their journey. They all received mana from heaven. They all drank water from a rock.

2 Peter 1:5-7 And beside this, giving all diligence, add to your faith virtue; and to virtue knowledge; And to knowledge temperance; and to temperance patience; and to patience godliness; And to godliness brotherly kindness; and to brotherly kindness charity.

2 Corinthians 13:5 Examine yourselves, whether ye be in the faith; prove your own selves. Know ye not your own selves, how that Jesus Christ is in you, except ye be reprobates?

First, the scripture calls for self examination. People are quick to examine other people and their circumstances. However, they are a bit slower when it comes to self examination. Secondly, the scripture calls for us to examine whether we are in the faith. What it doesn't call for is to examine if we are in line with the latest political or ecclesiastical hot point. Nor does it call for examination as to whether we have faith. The call is to be of <u>the</u> faith. You see there is a faith, there is some faith and then there is <u>the</u> faith. The word faith here is preceded by the definite article "the". This makes it a special specific faith that is being talked about. It reminds me of back in grade school we were taught there is a president and then there is *the* President.

Everyone has faith but everyone doesn't have faith in God. People have faith in the most unreliable things. I encourage everyone to have faith in God, and to examine whether the object of your faith is truly God. Let me explain. There are different things which can be the object of your faith. You can have faith in your status, your position, your church, your gifting or ability, your affiliations, your power, your quests, or a myriad number of things. None of these are particularly bad; but it is not the same as having faith in God. Faith in God allows you to hold on when or if your plans, ideas and dreams fail; because your faith is in God rather than any of these things. It also allows you to wait on the Lord. Sometimes, we have to wait to receive the promise. As the scriptures state; after having done the will of God we have need of patience. Have faith in God, rather than a particular outcome. Faith in God equates to a surety that God causes all things to work together for the good of all them that love him and are called according to his purpose. *(Romans 8:28)*.

Often we worry about a perceived outcome prior to experiencing any hardship. I've come to believe that we don't have to worry about the outcome when the source is pure. When we do things to please and obey God, in faith, we can leave the results up to him. It is amazing how often and easily we jettison hope and fully embrace fear.

Much too often, I have witnessed well-meaning believers allow their faith in God to morph into faith in their own faith. They started with faith in God. Somewhere along the way that turned into faith in themselves and their own desired outcome. Consider two biblical examples. God promised Abraham and Sarah a child. Then Sarah decided to help God out by giving Abraham her hand maiden for conception. So, I ask, is it possible that what they demonstrated faith in was the promise rather than the promiser? We believe *for* the promise. We believe *in* the promiser.

While I'm on the subject of faith, I want to take the time to state this concern and voice my plea. Because everyone has faith and it is easy to believe in something, it is also easy to have faith in one's faith. Faith in your faith is not the same thing as faith in God. Faith in your faith is earmarked by a belief that because you make a declaration, have a belief, or make a prediction; it makes that thing true. Truth is not just something you can depend on because you said it. Declarations of your ideas should not be the cornerstone of your faith.   Faith in God, allows one to make declarations, state beliefs, and make predictions because they are repeating what God has said. Do **not** exchange or mistake faith in God with faith in your faith. One of the reasons that the phenomenon of faith in faith has become so prevalent is because of how the scriptures are read and understood.

Matthew 9:22 But Jesus turned him about, and when he saw her, he said, Daughter, be of good comfort; thy faith hath made thee whole. And the woman was made whole from that hour.

This passage could be understood in one of two ways. It could be understood as the power of her faith or the object of her faith. I hold that it's the object of her faith that made her whole.

Acts 3:12,16 [12] And when Peter saw it, he answered unto the people, Ye men of Israel, why marvel ye at this? or why look ye so earnestly on us, as though by our own power or holiness we had made this man to walk? [16] And his name through faith in his name hath made this

man strong, whom ye see and know: yea, the faith which is by him hath given him this perfect soundness in the presence of you all. Here, Peter distinctly tells the people that it's not by the their own power rather it was faith in Jesus that made the man whole.

Let me further explain what I mean. When Shadrach, Meshach and Abednego faced the king, their response truly reflected their faith in God.

Shadrach, Meshach and Abednego exemplified faith in God. *Daniel 3:17-18 If it be so, our God whom we serve is able to deliver us from the burning fiery furnace, and he will deliver us out of thine hand, O king. [18] But if not, be it known unto thee, O king, that we will not serve thy gods, nor worship the golden image which thou hast set up.* It is evident in this scripture that they truly had faith (believed) that God was able and would eventually deliver them. "But if not" demonstrates that because of their faith in God, they were willing to forgo their desired outcome. Jesus is another example of having faith in God over a desire. *Matthew 26:39 And he went a little further, and fell on his face, and prayed, saying, O my Father, if it be possible, let this cup pass from me: nevertheless not as I will, but as thou wilt.* Putting aside any argument regarding Jesus' place in the Godhead, this passage is a glaring example to us of putting God's will ahead of our own and putting our faith in His will.

In essence, they were saying that God was fully able to miraculously deliver them. However, they went further to say that even if God did not deliver in that way, He would still deliver; even if it meant their death. The Bible has quite a number of examples of saints who had a sentence of death on their lives. Despite the death sentence, they believed in God. Queen Esther said "if I perish, I perish". When someone's faith is merely based on faith in their faith, they don't see beyond their expectation of how God will deliver. In other words, their expectation is in their faith rather than their God. Faith in faith is not the same as faith in God. When all hope is gone, faith in God allows one to hope beyond hope because one's hope is then in God alone. Their faith in God was not limited to determine what form the deliverance should take.

Ephesians 2:8 For by grace are ye saved through faith; and that not of yourselves: it is the gift of God:

According to this passage. We are saved by grace. I can't list the number of times I've heard that we are saved by faith. The truth is we are saved by grace. We aren't able to save ourselves. Faith is the vehicle by which we access God's salvation. We have to have faith in God to appropriate His free gift of salvation.

Job, who was a man who feared God and hated evil, uttered "Yea though he slay me, yet will I trust in him!"

Queen Esther when prompted to go before the king in intercession for Israel, at personal risk, went before the king with the utterance " if I perish, I perish. I'm going to see the king!"

Every one of these are examples of complete faith in God.

There is a place where discussion about faith revolves around faith as an action. This is inadequate. A more complete understanding of faith would involve faith as both action and subject. The full structure of faith involves faith as both action and subject. Our faith is in God, through the work of Christ Jesus.

Luke 17:4-5 And if he trespass against thee seven times in a day, and seven times in a day turn again to thee, saying, I repent; thou shalt forgive him. [5] And the apostles said unto the Lord, Increase our faith.

The Lord had just told the disciples that he required them to forgive those who repented of their trespass. Like many of us, when the offense is so great, they expressed that such an endeavor would be difficult. The only way they could see themselves fulfilling such a demand was if Jesus would help them by increasing their faith in Him. This amounts to increasing their dependence on Him.

I understand that there are some instances where you find it hard to obey the Lord. That is where your trust, faith, and dependence have to outweigh your fear, hate or doubt. This is where you have to perfect, complete or make your faith whole. Let's review the biblical example of blind Bartimaeus as we consider this.

Mark 10:46-49 And they came to Jericho: and as he went out of Jericho with his disciples and a great number of people, blind Bartimaeus, the son of Timaeus, sat by the highway side begging. [47] And when he heard that it was Jesus of Nazareth, he began to cry out, and say, Jesus, thou Son of David, have mercy on me. [48] And many charged him that he should hold his peace: but he cried

the more a great deal, Thou Son of David, have mercy on me. [49] And Jesus stood still, and commanded him to be called. And they call the blind man, saying unto him, Be of good comfort, rise; he calleth thee.

Out of his distress, Bartimaeus called out to the Lord. Voices responded to his call with a charge to be quiet. As you make application of this in your life, realize that there are times when you can identify with this man. Often the response to our cry comes from outsiders and ill wishers. However, sometimes that voice comes from our own head. Something within us tells us to give up, keep quiet, loose hope, and stop trying. The accusation is that the Lord is not concerned about you, nor does He hear you. The truth is, like Bartimaeus, the greater the distress, and the louder the external and internal voices, the greater our cry should be. The end of this encounter resulted in Jesus calling Bartimaeus to Himself.

It may seem paradoxical, but at times what I experience in myself and see in other believers is unbelief. There are times believers are believing God for some great miracle and waiting for it's manifestation with a fervent expectancy; yet have trouble believing God will supply their daily bread or meet some minor need. Conversely, there are some who believe God will meet their daily needs but can't perform the miraculous on their behalf. So, if in your self reflection, you find areas in which you have a hard time believing God; there are a couple things you should know. First, this unbelief in belief syndrome is more common than you may realize. Yet, like the remedy for sin, there is a solution.

Mark 9:23-24 KJV [23] Jesus said unto him, If thou canst believe, all things are possible to him that believeth. [24] And straightway the father of the child cried out, and said with tears, Lord, I believe; help thou mine unbelief. This passage relays the story of a man who went to Jesus in intercession for his son. So great was the son's affliction, that the father really had a hard time seeing how anyone could deliver his son; yet he was speaking to the Lord. Although Jesus calls out this doubt; causing the man to realize his unbelief, Jesus doesn't out right condemn the man. Instead, He corrects this father. Then the man acknowledges both, his belief and unbelief and asks Jesus to help him with his unbelief. Now, this is the point that I hope turns to encouragement for my readers. Be willing to take your petitions and requests to the Lord, even though your faith may be paradoxically mixed with unbelief. The key being that you do not settle with your doubt, but you give that doubt to the Lord. This might help. I have believed the Lord for some things and doubted in other things. One thing I have not doubted is God in Christ Jesus. So, that father in this passage believed the Lord. He had some hesitancy in believing what the Lord would do but had a sincere faith in the Lord.

There is one thing I want to clarify. The man's doubt was before he received a response from the Lord. This is why one of the things I promote is for each person to develop their own level of communication with the Lord. Once he heard the Lord's response, he believed the Lord would make good on fulfilling his request.

When we spend too much time entertaining doubt, without giving that doubt to the Lord, i fear we put ourselves in danger of the total collapse of our faith, and that is what the devil desires.

Luke 22:31-32 And the Lord said, Simon, Simon, behold, Satan hath desired to have you, that he may sift you as wheat: [32] But I have prayed for thee, that thy faith fail not: and when thou art converted, strengthen thy brethren.

There is another biblical example of one whom the devil sought to destroy their faith in God. When you read the story of Job, you will find the accounting of a man who feared God and hated evil. Satan's complaint to God against Job was that God had put a hedge about Job, insinuating that Job's faith in God was only because of God's blessings; and without such blessing Job would curse God, cementing his departure from faith in God. One of the most powerful verses in the Bible is ***Job 13:15-16 Though he slay me, yet will I trust in him: but I will maintain mine own ways before him. [16] He also shall be my salvation: for an hypocrite shall not come before him.***

Hardship can shake our faith. The unexpected and chaotic can reveal that one's faith was not well placed to begin with. However, there is a more subtle challenge to one's faith. Specifically, the failure to live up to one's faith. Simon Peter made a number of bold declarations concerning the strength of his faith and before the "cock crowed", he failed his self-proclamation on the strength of his faith three times. Jesus knew his lapse would occur before it happened. Jesus prayed for Peter prior to his apostatizing himself. Jesus prayed that when Satan would sift him, Peter's faith would not fail. Satan's role as accuser of the brethren, is one of the ways he sifts. You see, as he accuses, some of the things he says are true. We were guilty. We did fail. We did transgress. So, when Jesus prayed for Simon, He was praying that Peter would find the foundation of his faith and look toward Jesus. He failed, and this is often true for us today when our faith is in ourselves. He had faith in his own faith and ability. The Lord wanted Peter to shift the object of his faith from himself to the Lord. Therefore, his conversion was just that, being converted from one who was self-righteous to one who recognized Jehovah Tsidkenu (God is his righteousness). So, if you are reading this and struggled with the guilt of your past, and for some, truth be told, who struggle right now with the strength of their faith; have faith in God. Turn from your own righteousness or sense of failure and trust in Him. Consider Peter's journey. See if you can identify with him. Peter started as a fisherman, a regular Joe with a regular job. He then became a disciple, the staunchest, most zealous disciple. Then, in a moment of fear and uncertainty, Peter denied the Lord. Denied even knowing Him. He cursed so that witnesses would see that his behavior was uncharacteristic of a disciple. Then he wept. He grieved his denial of the Lord. In his grief, he cut himself off from the Lord. Jesus went to Peter, ministered to him and let him know that Jesus had a work for him. Did you see yourself in Peter's testimony? Have you denied the Lord in word or deed? Have you cut yourself off so that you no longer hear Him because you think you are no longer worthy? The truth is that none of us were ever worthy in ourselves. Our worth is inherent as a part of His creation. None of this is meant to diminish or wink at failures, especially one so important as denying the Lord. It is however about highlighting the fact that Peter's failure, the thing that Satan desired to sift, was his religious pride. Somewhere along the way, perhaps Peter's faith was in his own righteousness.

Perfect your faith. Mature it to the point that your faith is in God alone, not in your victories, not in your failures, just in God.

Let's examine one more selection of scripture as we try to grasp the essence of faith. **Luke 17:3-6 Take heed to yourselves: If thy brother trespass against thee, rebuke him; and if he repent, forgive him. [4] And if he trespass against thee seven times in a day, and seven times in a day turn again to thee, saying, I repent; thou shalt forgive him. [5] And the apostles said unto the Lord, Increase our faith. [6] And the Lord said, If ye had faith as a grain of mustard seed, ye might say unto this sycamine tree, Be thou plucked up by the root, and be thou planted in the sea; and it should obey you.** Jesus tells His disciples they must continually be ready to forgive a brother's trespass when he repents. The apostle's response was to ask the Lord to increase their faith. The Lord than compares faith to a mustard seed. He is teaching them that it is not the size or abundance of their faith, it is the quality of their faith. Precisely their faith has to be in Him. The disciples then ask Him to help them increase their faith. In essence it amounted to increasing their dependence on Him.

Chapter Six

Perfect Your Hope

Faith and hope are inextricably linked.

Hebrews 11:1 Now faith is the substance of things hoped for, the evidence of things not seen.

Romans 8:24-25 For we are saved by hope: but hope that is seen is not hope: for what a man seeth, why doth he yet hope for? [25] But if we hope for that we see not, then do we with patience wait for it.

Initially, hope is a wish for an unseen benefit. We stand in hope of receiving the promised blessing of a faithful God. We have need of patience and that patience is enveloped in hope. There is much evil and despair in the world, but there is also much joy and hope. There is a tendency for people to engage in self-diagnoses and prognosis. I don't think this is a problem in itself. However there are missteps that occur much too often. One is the tendency to lean toward one's own understanding and fail to seek counsel from someone with more knowledge, training and expertise. The other thing concerns prognosis of the projected outcome. It amazes me how people automatically go to the worst possible outcome, and act as if that is a given. When they gravitate to the worse scenario, they make no allowance for anything other than the very worst possible outcome. Every visit to the doctor is overshadowed by the fear of receiving pronouncement of some dreaded disease. Every visit to the boss's office is filled with dread. Every perceived threat is not just imagined in its worst possible outcome but acted on as if that outcome had already occurred and was written in stone. In my musings I wonder why. Why accept the worst case scenario as a forgone conclusion, without considering more favorable outcomes? Why not hope that the worst thing doesn't happen? I understand the truth of harsh trials in life. However, I believe the evil of the day is sufficient for itself. In other words, be more concerned with what is, instead of worrying about what might be. If you spend your resources (spiritual, mental, physical) on what is, you can often cut off what might be. Bad things do happen. As the saying goes, hope for the best and prepare for the worst. There is a way, however, that in preparing for the worst, there is no hope for the best. So, instead of automatically going to the worse, don't skip all the steps on the way to that fulfillment. In hope, expect something better. Then after passing through all those steps, deal with the inevitable. Just don't make it inevitable until it is so. If you choose to engage in trouble shooting or problem solving; you identify and solve one problem at a time. You don't burn the whole thing down. Well, some people handle bad news that way. They tend to burn the whole thing down rather than attempt to solve the problems one step at a time.

Lamentations 3:19-23 Remembering mine affliction and my misery, the wormwood and the gall. [20] My soul hath them still in remembrance, and is humbled in me. [21] This I recall to my mind, therefore have I hope. [22] It is of the Lord's mercies that we are not consumed, because his compassions fail not. [23] They are new every morning: great is thy faithfulness.

There is the kind of hope that king David demonstrated when he encountered the giant Goliath. His hope was under-girded by the memory of the victory God had given him over the lion and the bear. The hope displayed in the above Lamentation passage is reinforced by the author's memory of his affliction. To be more precise, it was the recollection of the Lord's mercies. The Lord's rich mercy and great faithfulness is offered daily in spite of one's failures, weaknesses and insecurities. Take hope that God who has already blessed in good times and bad, is able to do it again. You can hope in your current situation. Hope in God who has already moved in your behalf to bless and show His mercy.

Fear is something else that tends to stifle hope. When I counsel people who allow fear to paralyze them, I begin with assuring them that fear is a normal response, then go on to encourage to not remain in a state of fear.

Psalm 31:23-24 O love the LORD, all ye his saints: for the LORD preserveth the faithful, and plentifully rewardeth the proud doer. [24] Be of good courage, and he shall strengthen your heart, all ye that hope in the LORD.

Psalm 33:18-22 Behold, the eye of the LORD is upon them that fear him, upon them that hope in his mercy; [19] To deliver their soul from death, and to keep them alive in famine. [20] Our soul waiteth for the LORD: he is our help and our shield. [21] For our heart shall rejoice in him, because we have trusted in his holy name. [22] Let thy mercy, O LORD, be upon us, according as we hope in thee.

Acts 23:6 But when Paul perceived that the one part were Sadducees, and the other Pharisees, he cried out in the council, Men and brethren, I am a Pharisee, the son of a Pharisee: of the hope and resurrection of the dead I am called in question.

We live in hope of the resurrection. We have a lively hope. We have a hope of future glory. However, our hope is not just for the next life.

Mark 10:29-30 And Jesus answered and said, Verily I say unto you, There is no man that hath left house, or brethren, or sisters, or father, or mother, or wife, or children, or lands, for my sake, and the gospel's, [30] But he shall receive an hundredfold now in this time, houses, and brethren, and sisters, and mothers, and children, and lands, with persecutions; and in the world to come eternal life.

Our hope is not just for heaven; we hope and believe in the blessings and providence of a beneficent God. He blesses us with good things.

I have a practice that I engage in and encourage others to do. When despair would try to creep in and rob you of hope, think about the first time the worst thing you could imagine happened to you. Then remember how you made it through that time. Then remember the next time and each subsequent time after that; and remember how by the grace of God, each time you saw no reason to hope, somehow God brought you through. He sparks our hope and brings new life to our hope-lessness.

Acts 27:20-25 And when neither sun nor stars in many days appeared, and no small tempest lay on us, all hope that we should be saved was then taken away. [21] But after long abstinence Paul stood forth in the midst of them, and said, Sirs, ye should have hearkened unto me, and not have loosed from Crete, and to have gained this harm and loss. [22] And now I exhort you to be of good cheer: for there shall be no loss of any man's life among you, but of the ship. [23] For there stood by me this night the angel of God, whose I am, and whom I serve, [24] Saying, Fear not, Paul; thou must be brought before Caesar: and, lo, God hath given thee all them that sail with thee. [25]

Wherefore, sirs, be of good cheer: for I believe God, that it shall be even as it was told me.

If you have been in a storm for a long time and the tempest leads you to lose all hope in your salvation; understand you are not alone. This can apply both to your soul salvation as well as your situational salvation. Even the Apostle Paul reached the point where he felt that all hope was lost and he would probably perish at sea. Maybe we can learn something from Paul's experience. There is a path to take that allows us to escape the pull of hopelessness. Paul fasted, prayed, and sought the Lord. Having sought the Lord, the Lord instructed and comforted him. I believe the pivotal step Paul took to salvage hope was committing to seek the Lord. He was able to make such a step because he belonged to and served the Lord. If you belong to and serve the Lord, personal communication is open to you as well.

Another example comes to mind of a disciple or follower being caught in a storm. Peter walked on the water, only after he asked the Lord to bid him to come. He only began to sink, when he took his eyes off of Jesus. These two examples; Peter and Paul. Both of them losing hope while caught in a storm. One was out there because Jesus called him, the other out there because people set out in disobedience to a warning. Both had to commit to focusing on Jesus to keep from sinking. It didn't matter why they were there. The only thing that mattered was that they were there and they needed salvation to keep from sinking. That salvation was coming from Jesus.

Luke 24:17-21 And he said unto them, What manner of communications are these that ye have one to another, as ye walk, and are sad? [18] And the one of them, whose name was Cleopas, answering said unto him, Art thou only a stranger in Jerusalem, and hast not known the things which are come to pass there in these days? [19] And he said unto them, What things? And they said unto him, Concerning Jesus of Nazareth, which was a prophet mighty in deed and word before God and all the people: [20] And how the chief priests and our rulers delivered him to be condemned to death, and have crucified him. [21] But we trusted that it had been he which should have redeemed Israel: and beside all this, to day is the third day since these things were done.

These two disciples had hoped that Jesus would be the Messiah or deliverer; but then Jesus was crucified, and their hope was smashed. Jesus went through the scriptures to reveal himself in the scriptures to those disciples, and show that His crucifixion was necessary. I can't tell which of our storms are necessary and which are merely malicious. I do know that regardless of the source, which often inevitably leads to hopelessness; Jesus is the answer to our hope.

Hope on the mountaintop. Hope in the valley. Hope in the sunshine. Hope in the rain. Hope when all is well. Hope when all is in chaos. Hope in the sowing. Hope in the reaping. Hope when new things are created. Hope when old things are destroyed. Hope in life. Hope in death. Ultimately, hope in the Lord who is Lord of all.

CHAPTER SEVEN

PERFECT YOUR LOVE

THE BOND OF PERFECTNESS

Matthew 22:36-40 Master, which is the great commandment in the law? [37] Jesus said unto him, Thou shalt love the Lord thy God with all thy heart, and with all thy soul, and with all thy mind. [38] This is the first and great commandment. [39] And the second is like unto it, Thou shalt love thy neighbour as thyself. [40] On these two commandments hang all the law and the prophets.

Love is the greatest commandment. All of the other commandments hinge on loving God.

John 13:34-35 A new commandment I give unto you, That ye love one another; as I have loved you, that ye also love one another. [35] By this shall all men know that ye are my disciples, if ye have love one to another.

The scripture says that Jesus gave them a new commandment. I've often pondered what made this a new commandment. As the Old Testament book of Deuteronomy pointed out, there was always a requirement to love.

Deuteronomy 6:4-6 Hear, O Israel: The Lord our God is one Lord : [5] And thou shalt love the Lord thy God with all thine heart, and with all thy soul, and with all thy might. [6] And these words, which I command thee this day, shall be in thine heart.

I believe the word of God is always true. Therefore, there must be a way to resolve the prior command to love with this new commandment. Here is where the application takes on fresh meaning for us today as well as the Jews of Jesus' day. We have to have a new outlook and understanding of the centrality of love in our Christian walk. It is possible to attempt to follow the law with a sense of obligation, duty, and sacrifice; void of love. Our obligation, duty, and sacrifice should flow from and be empowered by love; love for God first, then love for our neighbor. The command in John 13 is to love as Jesus loved. We aren't to love in a selective way, limited to our tribe or selected few. We are to love our fellow man. Incidentally, God is not a misogynist, nor is He a feminist. Sometimes, when the Bible speaks of man, it's referring to mankind, the species. At other times, it's referring to the gender- an adult male. **Genesis 1:27 KJV So God created man in his own image, in the image of God created he him; male and female created he them.** God so loved the world that He gave His only begotten Son.

1 John 4:19-21 We love him, because he first loved us. [20] If a man say, I love God, and hateth his brother, he is a liar: for he that loveth not his brother whom he hath seen, how can he love God whom he hath not seen? [21] And this commandment have we from him, That he who loveth God love his brother also.

We have not been called to tear down our fellow man but to build them up. Our warfare is not against flesh and blood but against principalities and wickedness. When we are purveyors of evil, we become servants of the wicked one rather than an emissary of the holy one. According to this scripture passage, the demonstration of our love for one another is our witness to the world that we are of God. Consider the full implication of this. If we can't demonstrably live in love, the world is not able to identify us as belonging to the group of called out ones who are true Christians or followers of Christ. If you consider yourself a Christian; yet your heart is full of hatred, bigotry, and fear; maybe you should consider whether your claim is valid or actually self deception. If you are a believer yet struggle with anger issues; cry out to the Lord in faith. The unredeemed would rather justify and excuse their behavior than seek God for deliverance.

1 John 4:12-21 No man hath seen God at any time. If we love one another, God dwelleth in us, and his love is perfected in us. [13] Hereby know we that we dwell in him, and he in us, because he hath given us of his Spirit. [14] And we have seen and do testify that the Father sent

the Son to be the Saviour of the world. [15] Whosoever shall confess that Jesus is the Son of God, God dwelleth in him, and he in God. [16] And we have known and believed the love that God hath to us. God is love; and he that dwelleth in love dwelleth in God, and God in him. [17] Herein is our love made perfect, that we may have boldness in the day of judgment: because as he is, so are we in this world. [18] There is no fear in love; but perfect love casteth out fear: because fear hath torment. He that feareth is not made perfect in love. [19] We love him, because he first loved us. [20] If a man say, I love God, and hateth his brother, he is a liar: for he that loveth not his brother whom he hath seen, how can he love God whom he hath not seen? [21] And this commandment have we from him, That he who loveth God love his brother also.

As we live in God, our love grows more perfect. Think about that. The more we give our life to God, the stronger our love grows. There are areas in our lives that we might find difficult to relinquish to God. The more we hold on to and fail to yield to God, the more we lack love. Love requires sacrifice. Not always the kind of sacrifice that demands your blood and life, but the kind that requires overriding one's selfishness and acting on behalf and for the good of another or the general good. Furthermore, love overcomes fear. If God be for us, who can be against us? When we allow our love to mature, we understand that our love for Him is our response to His love for us. In His sovereignty, His providence and His love: we truly understand that He will never leave us or forsake us because He truly loves us, and we become confident because we accept and return that love.

As your love for God reflects an acknowledgement of His great love, it becomes easier to overcome fear. God is greater than all and the Most High God has His heart toward you. So, what should you fear? Your Father in heaven is greater than all and He loves you. Fear is a very real and powerful thing. It can be a paralyzing or coercive force.

Hebrews 2:15 And deliver them who through fear of death were all their lifetime subject to bondage.

People fear the unknown. People fear what tomorrow holds. They fear the imaginations of their own minds. They fear the threats of enemies, the machinations of associates, and betrayal by friends and loved ones. Fear is such a detrimental force, that it bears mentioning it here. Especially since the power that overcomes fear is love. In some circles, fear is taboo. In such circles, people are "afraid" to acknowledge their fear. They feel that such an acknowledgement is an affront to God. I hold that God is a better parent than any of us could ever be. When we have a child who is afraid of the dark, we don't yell at them, we comfort them. We might put a night light in their room. If a toddler is afraid of monsters hiding in the closet, we show them there are no monsters. If they are afraid of lightening, we might hold them to assuage their fear. So, if we fear, God comes along and says, "fear not". He doesn't condemn our fear, rather He comforts us and lets us know we don't have to fear because He has us covered.

Matthew 6:25-33 Therefore I say unto you, Take no thought for your life, what ye shall eat, or what ye shall drink; nor yet for your body, what ye shall put on. Is not the life more than meat, and the body than raiment? [26] Behold the fowls of the air: for they sow not, neither do they reap, nor gather into barns; yet your heavenly Father feedeth them. Are ye not much better than they? [27] Which of you by taking thought can add one cubit unto his stature? [28] And why take ye thought for raiment? Consider the lilies of the field, how they grow; they toil not, neither do they spin: [29] And yet I say unto you, That even Solomon in all his glory was not arrayed like one of these. [30] Wherefore, if God so clothe the grass of the field, which to day is, and to morrow is cast into the oven, shall he not much more clothe you, O ye of little faith? [31] Therefore take no thought, saying, What shall we eat? or, What shall we drink? or, Wherewithal shall we be clothed? [32] (For after all these things do the Gentiles seek:) for your heavenly Father knoweth that ye have need of all these things. [33] But seek ye first the kingdom of God, and his righteousness; and all these things shall be added unto you.

The degree to which we let fear overcome us, is the degree to which we are not fully convinced of the love of God.

1 Corinthians 13:1-13 Though I speak with the tongues of men and of angels, and have not charity, I am become as sounding brass, or a tinkling cymbal. [2] And though I have the gift of prophecy, and understand all mysteries, and all knowledge; and though I have all faith, so that I could remove mountains, and have not charity, I am nothing. [3] And though I bestow all my goods to feed the poor , and though I give my body to be burned, and have not charity, it profiteth me nothing. [4] Charity suffereth long, and is kind; charity envieth not; charity vaunteth not itself, is not puffed up, [5] Doth not behave itself unseemly, seeketh not her own, is not easily provoked, thinketh no evil; [6] Rejoiceth not in iniquity, but rejoiceth in the truth; [7] Beareth all things, believeth all things, hopeth all things, endureth all things. [8] Charity never faileth: but whether there be prophecies, they shall fail; whether there be tongues, they shall cease; whether there be knowledge, it shall vanish away. [9] For we know in part, and we prophesy in part. [10] But when that which is perfect is come, then that which is in part shall be done away. [11] When I was a child, I spake as a child, I understood as a child, I thought as a child: but when I became a man, I put away childish things. [12] For now we see through a glass, darkly; but then face to face: now I know in part; but then shall I know even as also I am known. [13] And now abideth faith, hope, charity, these three; but the greatest of these is charity.

You can't justify your lack of love while hiding behind some thinly veiled act of hatred. We are all familiar with the saying "actions speak louder than words". If we say that we are Christians and do not practice love, we prove ourselves liars. It is our demonstration and practice of love which gives evidence and lends credence to our discipleship. Without such demonstration, the world cannot know that we are disciples or followers of Christ. If we are not disciples, we are not Christians.

Luke 10:25-29 And, behold, a certain lawyer stood up, and tempted him, saying, Master, what shall I do to inherit eternal life? [26] He said unto him, What is written in the law? how readest thou? [27] And he answering said, Thou shalt love the Lord thy God with all thy heart, and with all thy soul, and with all thy strength, and with all thy mind; and thy neighbour as thyself. [28] And he said unto him, Thou hast answered right: this do, and thou shalt live. [29] But he, willing to justify himself, said unto Jesus, And who is my neighbour?

Jesus continued His dialogue with describing a man who was waylaid along the road to Jericho. He mentioned the three individuals that came across the injured man along with their response to the situation.

Luke 10:36-37 Which now of these three, thinkest thou, was neighbour unto him that fell among the thieves? [37] And he said, He that shewed mercy on him. Then said Jesus unto him, Go, and do thou likewise.

The import of the identity and response of each of the participants was no small thing, and was probably not lost on the lawyer Jesus was talking to. One of the participants had more important things to do. Another did not want to be tainted by the uncleanness of the victim. The third belonged to an ostracized class. Another passage lets us know the Jews had no dealings with the Samaritans. Yet only one of these acted like a neighbour, the Samaritan. Only one acted in love. How many times do we neglect an opportunity to demonstrate love because we have something else to do, or simply because it would cost us something. Maybe the opportunity is lost because we don't want to be marred by what we perceive as their physical or ethnic uncleanness. Maybe we won't show love because the recipient belongs to a class with whom we refuse to have any dealings.

Matthew 24:10-13 And then shall many be offended, and shall betray one another, and shall hate one another. [11] And many false prophets shall rise, and shall deceive many. [12] And because iniquity shall abound, the love of many shall wax cold. [13] But he that shall endure unto the end, the same shall be saved.

The world has given us a perverted view of justice. Many think of justice as just what is good for them. Furthermore, many replace justice with vengeance. One of the reasons why this form of hatred is so effective is because of its subtilty. People are angry because there is reason to be angry. Iniquity, sin, trespasses, offenses and evil have increased in the world. It seems as if injustice rules and people want to correct the injustice. The problem is that those who want to be champions of justice often become purveyors of injustice when they act out of hatred. One huge step in perfecting your love is to do your deeds from a heart of love rather than hate.

1 Peter 1:22 Seeing ye have purified your souls in obeying the truth through the Spirit unto unfeigned love of the brethren, see that ye love one another with a pure heart fervently:

It is relatively easy to smile, offer up platitudes and say I love you. Love in truth, not just with words. I want to take a few moments to talk about what love is not. In our zeal to fulfill the command, there are some things we should understand. To misunderstand may cause us to demonstrate the opposite of our intention – hate. It is not love to enable self destruction. It is not love to enable and be complicit in wrong doing. It is not love to watch someone run off a cliff and jump into the abyss without giving warning.

Ezekiel 3:18-19 When I say unto the wicked, Thou shalt surely die; and thou givest him not warning, nor speakest to warn the wicked from his wicked way, to save his life; the same wicked man shall die in his iniquity; but his blood will I require at thine hand. [19] Yet if thou warn the wicked, and he turn not from his wickedness, nor from his wicked way, he shall die in his iniquity; but thou hast delivered thy soul.

Psalm 23:4 Yea, though I walk through the valley of the shadow of death, I will fear no evil: for thou art with me; thy rod and thy staff they comfort me.

Love includes discipline and correction, not purely punishment. Withholding correction or instruction, what passes as love can become enablement for the basest inclinations of the heart. Without the love of God, it can be difficult to walk the fine line between discipline and punishment, correction and control, and encouraging and enabling. It takes true love for God and His wisdom to love in truth. Endeavor to do so.

CHAPTER EIGHT

PERFECT YOUR WARFARE

FIGHT THE GOOD FIGHT

1 Timothy 6:12 Fight the good fight of faith, lay hold on eternal life, whereunto thou art also called, and hast professed a good profession before many witnesses. Without question, a great spiritual battle is raging. I want to encourage God's people to perfect their warfare. I have identified several things that interfere or compromise our warfare. The first is that some do not acknowledge that there is indeed a war going on. If we deny warfare is upon us, we leave ourselves vulnerable to the enemy. We can close our eyes, turn our back, and proverbially put our head in the sand and surrender to the enemy of our soul; or we can engage. If we settle for things as they are, we perish. *2 Kings 7:3 And there were four leprous men at the entering in of the gate: and they said one to another, Why sit we here until we die?* Choosing not to engage is akin to sitting down and waiting to die, instead of choosing life. Some people are getting ready for war; not realizing that war is already upon them. We have an enemy to our soul. One who has come to kill, steal and destroy. This enemy is a deceiver. One who would, if it were possible, deceive the very elect of God. I implore you to get involved in the battle. Don't just sit still and die. Get engaged in the battle.

Besides the failure to see and understand that we are engaged in spiritual warfare, there are also those who are fighting the wrong battle. There are some who refuse to fight at all. Realize that there is a war raging. The days are evil. Scrimmages of injustice do occur, as we await the unfolding of justice to be revealed. Some people fight against people with whom they either disagree or dislike. ***Ephesians 6:12 For we wrestle not against flesh and blood, but against principalities, against powers, against the rulers of the darkness of this world, against spiritual wickedness in high places.***

Once you decide to get involved in the battle, you then have to understand the nature of the battle that is raging. Too many people fight the wrong battle. Disciples wanted to burn down a village in Luke 9:54-55. A crowd attempted to stone a woman caught in adultery in John chapter 8. People are quick to fight in the latest cultural wars. "Patriots" fight against the Mexicans, Haitians, Chinese, Japanese, Koreans, Jews, or any foreign national. In politics, Republicans fight against Democrats, and conservatives fight against liberals.

Now, I'm about to say something and I want you to pay close attention. There are some whose first response will be one of incredulity. Many are so involved with battling the devil, they miss an important aspect of battle. The importance of battle is not just what we are fighting against, but what we are fighting for! Fighting against the devil is only fighting half the battle. We fight for the faith. We fight to live by faith. We contend earnestly for the faith. ***Jude 1:3 Beloved, when I gave all diligence to write unto you of the common salvation, it was needful for me to write unto you, and exhort you that ye should earnestly contend for the faith which was once delivered unto the saints.*** When Jude endeavored to write about salvation, he felt it needful to write about struggling or contending for the faith. He didn't talk about the struggle against the devil! It is a stand for the truth that stands against falsehood. It is unclear whether Jude intended to make his exhortation part of his discourse on their common salvation, or he intended one thing and was prompted to go down a different path. In either case, he strongly urged his readers to contend or fight for the true faith. More true believers have to stand for the true faith. There are quite a number of religious systems floating around, that may represent the fulness of the gospel in part, in whole, or not at all. The dying world needs the truth of the gospel of Jesus Christ. I find this amazing but some in their selfish zeal, present something all together different. They don't fight for the faith.

1 Timothy 6:10-12 For the love of money is the root of all evil: which while some coveted after, they have erred from the faith, and pierced themselves through with many sorrows. [11] But thou, O man of God, flee these things; and follow after righteousness, godliness, faith, love, patience, meekness. [12] Fight the good fight of faith, lay hold on eternal life, whereunto thou art also called, and hast professed a good profession before many witnesses.

Luke 9:49-56 And John answered and said, Master, we saw one casting out devils in thy name; and we forbad him, because he followeth not with us. [50] And Jesus said unto him, Forbid him not: for he that is not against us is for us. [51] And it came to pass, when the time was come that he should be received up, he stedfastly set his face to go to Jerusalem, [52] And sent messengers before his face: and they went, and entered into a village of the Samaritans, to make ready for him. [53] And they did not receive him, because his face was as though he would go to Jerusalem. [54] And when his disciples James and John saw this, they said, Lord, wilt thou that we command fire to come down from heaven, and consume them, even as Elias did? [55] But he turned, and rebuked them, and said, Ye know not what manner of spirit ye are of. [56] For the Son of man is not come to destroy men's lives, but to save them. And they went to another village.

The first part of this passage is about disciples who wanted to fight against others who were raging war against the devil simply because they were not a part of their group. I submit that this scenario occurs too often, even in this day and age. Followers of one group war against another, and it's not because of their doing evil. In fact, they were actively casting out the devil. The second part involved disciples seeking to destroy the lives of others. The context of this exchange is interesting. Jesus sent some disciples into a Samaritan village ahead of His arrival. When Jesus arrived, the Samaritans refused to hear Him, when they realized He was set to go to Jerusalem. According to **John 4:9**, the Jews had no dealings with the Samaritans. In light of this, the Samaritans were unwilling to listen to someone who was on their way to visit those who had ostracized them. This was not a good thing. They lost an opportunity to hear the gospel. The disciple's response was far worse than the Samaritans. They wanted to call down fire from heaven and burn up the people. They were fighting the wrong war. Instead of fighting against ignorance of the truth, they wanted to destroy people's lives. They justified themselves, no doubt, thinking precedent for calling down fire had been set by Elijah and by them following suit, they would be doing God a favor. The Lord's rebuke was sharp. They were fighting the wrong war, and in doing so, they were antithetical to the spirit of God.

Although many choose the wrong battle, make no mistake about it, war is upon us. Fight the good fight. As battles go, there are a lot of battles in which we can engage. The late civil rights activist and Congressman John Lewis talked about getting in "good trouble". There are good fights, but not all fights are good. In some ways, this chapter is a call to take up arms, putting on the whole armor of God. It is also about being strategic and discerning in choosing which battles to undertake. Once we understand the true nature of our warfare and choose to fight the right battle; we then have to put on the correct armor.

1 Samuel 17:38-39,45 And Saul armed David with his armour, and he put an helmet of brass upon his head; also he armed him with a coat of mail. [39] And David girded his sword upon his armour, and he assayed to go; for he had not proved it. And David said unto Saul, I cannot go with these; for I have not proved them. And David put them off him. [45] Then said David to the Philistine, Thou comest to me with a sword, and with a spear, and with a shield: but I come to thee in the name of the LORD of hosts, the God of the armies of Israel, whom thou hast defied.

David had to choose the right armor. David had not tried and proven the king's armor. Saul's armor would not be effective for David. The world's armor and weapons are not effective against the world. It takes the armament of the spirit to confound and destroy the works of the devil.

Ephesians 6:13-18 Wherefore take unto you the whole armour of God, that ye may be able to withstand in the evil day, and having done all, to stand. [14] Stand therefore, having your loins girt about with truth, and having on the breastplate of righteousness; [15] And your feet shod with the preparation of the gospel of peace; [16] Above all, taking the shield of faith, wherewith ye shall be able to quench all the fiery darts of the wicked. [17] And take the helmet of salvation, and the sword of the Spirit, which is the word of God: [18] Praying always with all prayer and supplication in the Spirit, and watching thereunto with all perseverance and supplication for all saints;

2 Timothy 4:7 I have fought a good fight, I have finished my course, I have kept the faith:

Chapter Nine

PERFECT YOUR HUMILITY

Not by Pride

James 4:6-7,10 But he giveth more grace. Wherefore he saith, God resisteth the proud, but giveth grace unto the humble. [7] Submit yourselves therefore to God. Resist the devil, and he will flee from you. [10] Humble yourselves in the sight of the Lord, and he shall lift you up.

Hubris. There is so much pride in the hearts of men. Hubris is excessive pride and self-confidence.

Daniel 4:30-32 The king spake, and said, Is not this great Babylon, that I have built for the house of the kingdom by the might of my power, and for the honour of my majesty? [31] While the word was in the king's mouth, there fell a voice from heaven, saying, O king Nebuchadnezzar, to thee it is spoken; The kingdom is departed from thee. [32] And they shall drive thee from men, and thy dwelling shall be with the beasts of the field: they shall make thee to eat grass as oxen, and seven times shall pass over thee, until thou know that the most High ruleth in the kingdom of men, and giveth it to whomsoever he will.

Nebuchadnezzar was an example of someone who let his pride rule him, and as a result, God moved against him. Pride is no minor thing. Hubris, excessive pride, can cause God to resist you. It's one thing for God to allow certain things or to refrain from certain actions, and quite another for God to move in resistance to your prideful acts. I encourage each one to keep your hubris in check, lest God is prompted to move against you in His resistance. More than once I've seen people boast that they created their wealth or position by their own hand. They have looked over their small empire and basked in their own importance. I only caution that you be aware and avoid this pitfall.

Proverbs 16:18 Pride goeth before destruction, and an haughty spirit before a fall.

Proverbs 29:23 A man's pride shall bring him low: but honour shall uphold the humble in spirit.

2 Kings 5:13 And his servants came near, and spake unto him, and said, My father, if the prophet had bid thee do some great thing, wouldest thou not have done it? how much rather then, when he saith to thee, Wash, and be clean?

This passage regards Namaan, a mighty man of valor who was a Syrian and a leper. Being a mighty man of valor, he didn't want to undertake some small quest to obtain the blessing of

God. I suspect that his pride and ego were involved. If he had undertaken some great task, there was the possibility that he could get some glory by accomplishing a great feat. His submission to bathe in the river Nile proved that it was nothing of his greatness. The procurement of his blessing was solely by the power and will of God.

2 Chronicles 7:14 If my people, which are called by my name, shall humble themselves, and pray, and seek my face, and turn from their wicked ways; then will I hear from heaven, and will forgive their sin, and will heal their land.

Demonstration of power with God and man hinges on humility. It is a given, that such power is reserved for God's people, the people who are called by and follow the name of Christ. These Christians have to be willing to humble themselves and pray to their father in heaven. It is then that God hears them and moves on their behalf.

1 Peter 5:5-6 Likewise, ye younger, submit yourselves unto the elder. Yea, all of you be subject one to another, and be clothed with humility: for God resisteth the proud, and giveth grace to the humble. [6] Humble yourselves therefore under the mighty hand of God, that he may exalt you in due time:

Often, we are unable to see the move of God. It could be because we have not humbled ourselves. We have not submitted our way, will, desires, and actions to please Him rather than ourselves. Hence we fail to pray to Him. Alternatively, we call our demands prayer. This shouldn't be the norm but it does happen.

1 Corinthians 1:23-24 But we preach Christ crucified, unto the Jews a stumblingblock, and unto the Greeks foolishness; [24] But unto them which are called, both Jews and Greeks, Christ the power of God, and the wisdom of God.

Have you ever asked , "why a stumbling block?" What is it that causes people to stumble? They stumble at the paradox that what seems weak is actually strong. Those who valued martial power and victory could not fathom that the Messiah was a convicted (falsely) felon who died on a tree. Those who valued wisdom could not fathom that a stranger from Galilee who preached, what seemed to them to be foolishness, was actually the express image of the invisible God. They could not accept that the deliverer would not deliver himself. The great physician would not heal himself. In new testament days, many refused to accept a humble savior. Today some refuse to accept the crucified Christ because to do so would mandate that they would have to put themselves on the proverbial cross and also be willing to humble themselves.

Luke 18:10-14 Two men went up into the temple to pray; the one a Pharisee, and the other a publican. [11] The Pharisee stood and prayed thus with himself, God, I thank thee, that I am not as other men are, extortioners, unjust, adulterers, or even as this publican. [12] I fast twice in the week, I give tithes of all that I possess. [13]

And the publican, standing afar off, would not lift up so much as his eyes unto heaven, but smote upon his breast, saying, God be merciful to me a sinner. [14] I tell you, this man went down to his house justified rather than the other: for every one that exalteth himself shall be abased; and he that humbleth himself shall be exalted.

Two men went into the temple to pray. One prayed citing his righteousness. As you read that passage you can sense the immense level of self righteous pride that man felt. The other man only confessed his sinful nature and pled for the mercy of God. One was prideful, the other was humble. Only one was justified. Make your petitions to God but do so with an air of humility before the most high God. Smith Wigglesworth, a great Pentecostal evangelist of the twentieth century who performed miracles, attributed his demonstration of the power of God to humility. **In this** passage the Pharisee was not a bad person. In fact, his boast was in how perfectly he kept the law. He went beyond what was required. He didn't fast once a week, he fasted twice a week. He didn't just give a tenth of his produce, he gave a tenth of all of his possessions. He didn't do any of the bad things and went over and above in doing the good things. This passage begins with *Luke 18:9 And he spake this parable unto certain which trusted in themselves that they were righteous, and despised others:* The secret to walking in the power of God is humility. It's not the brand of humility that always yells "woe is me". There is a level of self degradation which actually denies that God is able to move in your life.

1 Peter 5:5-7 Likewise, ye younger, submit yourselves unto the elder. Yea, all of you be subject one to another, and be clothed with humility: for God resisteth the proud, and giveth grace to the humble. [6] Humble yourselves therefore under the mighty hand of God, that he may exalt you in due time: [7] Casting all your care upon him; for he careth for you.

Many people, regardless of their station in life have a sense of class distinction or some sort of hierarchy. The issues of leadership, authority and responsibility aside; we are truly called to submit to one another. We should be willing and prepared to forgo our sense of supremacy in order to submit to God. God can use anybody and anything to fulfill His purpose. God used a donkey to warn a prophet, and a raven to feed another. When we let class status cause us to look down on others, there are two things we allow to perpetuate: One is we cut off an avenue whereby God might speak to us. The other is that we can look down on the image of God in our neighbor.

Humble yourself under God and He will exalt you. God can humble us or we can choose to humble ourselves.

Zechariah 4:6 Then he answered and spake unto me, saying, This is the word of the Lord unto Zerubbabel, saying, Not by might, nor by power, but by my spirit, saith the Lord of hosts.

You see, it's not by your power (or importance), not by your might (or weakness). It's all through the power of the Holy Spirit.

Proverbs 6:16-17 These six things doth the Lord hate: yea, seven are an abomination unto him: [17] A proud look, a lying tongue, and hands that shed innocent blood,

The first thing listed in the things God hates is pride. Pride basically is the focus on one's self. It is relatively easy for us to notice someone who has a high level of self esteem. However, I present another scenario for you. What about the individual who is drowning in low self esteem? The person with a high self esteem and the person with a low self esteem are different sides of the same coin. The operative word is self. The enemy is very subtle. Most people easily identify the blowhard as a self centered individual who makes everything revolve around himself. False humility is a term I use to describe the scenario which involves the individual boasting in their sense of worthlessness. In both scenarios the person is focused on a sense of self. I believe the enemy of our soul uses both sides of this proverbial coin. To the one, he influences their sense of self worth to steal the glory from God and claim it for themselves. For those on the other side of the coin; he amplifies their self loathing so that they only see their weaknesses and frailties, and never truly accept the power of God. The one that loudly complains about their trials, like the proud person, is saying look at me. I call it false humility because it screams – me. True humility would say although I am going through my trials, look at my God who is able to sustain and bring me through.

Psalm 121:1-2 I will lift up mine eyes unto the hills, from whence cometh my help. [2] My help cometh from the LORD, which made heaven and earth.

An integral part of spiritual growth involves exchanging that proverbial coin, the one with self etched on both sides, for a different form of currency, one with God as the guarantor. The person whose trade is in the "self coin" has not yet learned to cast their cares upon Him. They often either don't go to him because they don't realize their need for Him, or they feel their predicament is beyond His reach and concern. There is a reason the scriptures say not many mighty and noble are called. It's because the mighty think they are sufficient within themselves. Alternatively, the weak and frail know they have no strength. No matter how often I say it's not about your weakness or strength, somebody's response is that I don't understand that they are truly without strength and therefore incapable of performing. I don't argue such an assessment. My point is that it is not about your strength. It is about His.

Chapter Ten
PERFECT YOUR KNOWLEDGE

Wisdom and knowledge. Although Wisdom and knowledge are distinct, they are inextricably linked. Knowledge is obtaining information. Wisdom is the prudent application of knowledge. It is important to grow in our wisdom and knowledge. The scriptures give testimony to the importance of knowledge when the declaration is made through the prophet Hosea:

My people are destroyed for lack of knowledge: because thou hast rejected knowledge, I will also reject thee, that thou shalt be no priest to me: seeing thou hast forgotten the law of thy God, I will also forget thy children. (Hosea 4:6)

People die every day. Those that lack the knowledge of how to obtain eternal life perish eternally. Some don't know they can have eternal life. Others don't know how to obtain such life. Just as this entire topic of perfection has a beginning, so too does the particular issue of knowledge. ***Proverbs 1:7 The fear of the Lord is the beginning of knowledge: but fools despise wisdom and instruction.*** Knowledge or knowing begins with the fear of the Lord. The "fear of the Lord" can be defined as reverential awe of the Lord. God, the creator of life is the source of knowledge and wisdom.

Acts 17:23 For as I passed by, and beheld your devotions, I found an altar with this inscription, TO THE UNKNOWN GOD. Whom therefore ye ignorantly worship, him declare I unto you.

We should begin with the knowledge of God. Many people have no knowledge of God. Surprisingly, however, there are some Christian and other religious people who worship an unknown God. The God that they worship does not match the God of creation. God spoke and created the cosmos ex nihilo (out of nothing). God who offered up His only begotten Son. God who loved the world. God who is just, holy and righteous. For those who question, the veracity of my statements, consider the following examples. Consider those who learn about all the rituals that pertain to their organization but fail to put as much effort into learning about the God that is purported to be the head of the organization.

There is a challenge I offer that highlights one's understanding of who God is. There are people who will walk into an establishment. If for some reason they are not satisfied with the service they will ask for the manager. If they are not satisfied with the manager, some will take it further and ask to speak with the owner. If they don't get satisfaction there, they will take it further. For those establishments which are part of a corporation, the customer might even go to the corporate office to get satisfaction. The point is this: they go past all the middle management and go to the head. We should have that kind of initiative when comes to our relationship with God. Skip all the middle management and go directly to God. If we are to go to Him, we have to know that God is. I've heard from people on a quest to uncover great mysteries and others who relished in the prospect of gaining great power.

Romans 10:2-3 For I bear them record that they have a zeal of God, but not according to knowledge. [3] For they being ignorant of God's righteousness, and going about to establish their own righteousness, have not submitted themselves unto the righteousness of God.

Zeal without knowledge and knowledge bereft of wisdom. This is where many find themselves as they settle for the fervency of their zeal in lieu of walking in integrity. It's great to have passion and zeal but seek to understand what you are passionate about and identify the object of your zeal. Paul laid out a complaint that his countrymen had zeal. However they did not have knowledge of God. This applies to many people today. Too many substitute the high prize of a knowledge of God with a much weaker zeal for God. Not that zeal is inherently meager. It's just that it is akin to basking in the idea of a loving relationship without experiencing a loving relationship. Don't settle for mere rhetoric when you can enjoy partaking of the substance.

Many have faith but are unable to articulate what they believe. I don't intend to degrade or diminish anyone who can't articulate their ideology. I actually believe that it is rare, if possible, to fully understand or articulate; because we are growing in the infinite wisdom of who He is. Instead, I intend to propose a remedy that we don't become stymied in zeal. It can become easy to announce a vague "I just believe". Then when some acquire knowledge, they lack the ability to appropriately and effectively use their knowledge to transform it to wisdom.

The failure to acquire wisdom and knowledge leads to the formation of a skewed form of righteousness. This righteousness is not the righteousness of God. The righteousness of God revolves around God the father and the express image of the invisible God; Christ Jesus.

So, don't be content with your zeal, your passion, your ecstasy in Christ. Undergird that passion with knowledge

Philippians 3:8 Yea doubtless, and I count all things but loss for the excellency of the knowledge of Christ Jesus my Lord: for whom I have suffered the loss of all things, and do count them but dung, that I may win Christ.

Paul made the knowledge of Christ the preeminent thing. Listen, I'm not against learning about great mysteries or church ordinances and doctrines or all about the works and workers of darkness in this world. I just encourage that the knowledge of God does not lack, and hold a lower place of interest and importance. Paul treated everything else as garbage in comparison to the knowledge of God. So, I encourage you to grow. Learn all you can about everything you can. Learn about powers and principalities. Learn about church doctrine. Learn about the hidden things God reveals. Make sure that in all your learning, first and foremost you learn about God and in particularly the express image of the invisible sovereign God – Jesus Christ.

2 Peter 3:17-18 Ye therefore, beloved, seeing ye know these things before, beware lest ye also, being led away with the error of the wicked, fall from your own stedfastness. [18] But grow in grace, and in the knowledge of our Lord and Saviour Jesus Christ. To him be glory both now and for ever. Amen.

Growing in the knowledge of the Lord necessitates that we grow in knowing Him. You see, many people know about Him but they don't know Him. To be fair, we should note that at one time, we had no knowledge of Jesus. Then we learned about Him. As we build our relationship, we develop an intimate knowledge of him. It's that way with our physical relationships. For those of you with a special someone in your life; there was a time you did not know that person. At some point you said I am going to get to know that person. Then that knowledge became experiential intimate knowledge. So too, Jesus says we are to take up His yoke and learn of Him. Consider one of the lessons we can learn from the incident with the rich young ruler in Matthew 19. The man came to Jesus asking what did he lack for salvation. Jesus' ultimate response was for him to give up everything he had and follow Jesus. That young man knew about Jesus, whom he called good master and he knew about the law which he believed he followed, but he did not **know** Jesus. This was proven by his own sense of lack. This was also corroborated by Jesus' response to him culminating in direction for the man to give up all and follow Him.

According to conventional wisdom, when we think about knowledge, we think about knowing facts, or ideas, or people, or rules or laws, or some such thing.

Consider the following biblical references.

1 Corinthians 12:1 Now concerning spiritual gifts, brethren, I would not have you ignorant.

2 Timothy 2:15 Study to shew thyself approved unto God, a workman that needeth not to be ashamed, rightly dividing the word of truth.

John 8:31-32 Then said Jesus to those Jews which believed on him, If ye continue in my word, then are ye my disciples indeed; [32] And ye shall know the truth, and the truth shall make you free.

These scriptures don't just teach of the importance of growing in the knowledge of the word. They also infer a direct relationship of knowledge of the word with the knowledge of God, and Jesus is the revelation of God.

CHAPTER ELEVEN

PERFECT YOUR WALK

Don't just talk the talk. Walk the walk. People can learn the language of Christendom.

Mimicking the key phrases in the Christian church does not mean that the individual is living according to Christian doctrine. Everyone has a system of beliefs. Sometimes they cannot define what they believe. Which in turn makes it difficult to walk in integrity. One of my brothers used to often say, " I just believe God". That prompted me one day to respond, "What is it that you believe about God because you aren't living anything?" Dear reader, I ask of you – what is it that you believe about God? What you truly believe is reflected by how you live.

Luke 6:46 And why call ye me, Lord, Lord, and do not the things which I say?

Jesus was challenging them to not just talk the talk but to walk the walk

James 2:18 Yea, a man may say, Thou hast faith, and I have works: shew me thy faith without thy works, and I will shew thee my faith by my works.

James addresses the argument revolving around how we demonstrate our faith. The argument he makes is, it is futile to say you have faith, if you don't walk out that faith by what you do and how you live. The way we live reveals what we truly believe. This scripture reference and the next isn't about working for salvation. They are about how we live out our life in Christ.

Philippians 2:12-13 Wherefore, my beloved, as ye have always obeyed, not as in my presence only, but now much more in my absence, work out your own salvation with fear and trembling. [13] For it is God which worketh in you both to will and to do of his good pleasure.

You work out your salvation by allowing the will of God to work in your life and act accordingly. When you accept the gift of God which is Christ in you, The Holy Spirit is at work in you. If Christ is indeed in you, live out that relationship. God is at work in you. The Holy Spirit works in you to fulfill the good pleasure of God.

Psalm 86:11 Teach me thy way, O Lord ; I will walk in thy truth: unite my heart to fear thy name.

After learning the ways of the Lord, we actually have to walk in His ways.

Deuteronomy 10:12 And now, Israel, what doth the Lord thy God require of thee, but to fear the Lord thy

God, to walk in all his ways, and to love him, and to serve the Lord thy God with all thy heart and with all thy soul, Galatians 5:25 If we live in the Spirit, let us also walk in the Spirit.

There are some endeavors we undertake which are done passively. Others are done proactively. Take something as simple as breathing. Prior to my lung transplant, I was on supplemental oxygen. At times, my breathing was passive. Didn't take much effort or thought. There were other times when the act of breathing was done proactively. It took concentration and a great deal of effort. You might be able to identify areas in your life where you can distinguish between proactivity and passivity. You might even identify with my example of breathing. When it comes to walking in the spirit, it should be done passively and actively. There are situations where our walk should just flow. You walk based on your character and core beliefs. It doesn't take much thought or effort. There are other times when it takes a great deal of thought and effort. You have to discern where your wheel well is and stay in your lane. You have to learn how to seek God for His direction. Then follow that leading whether it be easy or hard.

Proverbs 16:25 There is a way that seemeth right unto a man, but the end thereof are the ways of death.

Some seek the easy way. Surprisingly, some seek the hard way. It doesn't matter if your path is easy or hard. The only thing that matters is that you walk in the path that the Lord has prepared for you, and trust in God for the results.

Jeremiah 29:11 For I know the thoughts that I think toward you, saith the Lord, thoughts of peace, and not of evil, to give you an expected end.

Contextually, God had given this word to Jeremiah to encourage his people to go into bondage. God still had plans to bless them.

Isaiah 30:20-21 And though the Lord give you the bread of adversity, and the water of affliction, yet shall not thy teachers be removed into a corner any more, but thine eyes shall see thy teachers: [21] And thine ears shall hear a word behind thee, saying, This is the way, walk ye in it, when ye turn to the right hand, and when ye turn to the left.

A great impediment to having a mature walk in the Lord involves the vanity of words. Solomon complained that all was vanity. Words become vain or empty when they are just words and do not truly reflect belief or intent. Words can also be vain or empty when they reflect a sincere belief but still lead to destruction. So, I recommend doing two things to facilitate a complete, whole and perfect walk in Christ. Both involve some degree of self-reflection. You may have to work at having your deed follow your word. You fully and truly believe something when your actions follow your word. That point where acts do not follow thoughts or words is the point where the idea represented by those words should be examined. Secondly, the beliefs have to be correct. Otherwise the ultimate outcome is death.

Luke 6:46-47 And why call ye me, Lord, Lord, and do not the things which I say? [47] Whosoever cometh to me, and heareth my sayings, and doeth them, I will shew you to whom he is like:

An impediment lies in when one starts to let their words stand in place of their actions. They can become complacent and not work to solidify their words with some meaningful action.

Matthew 7:24-27 Therefore whosoever heareth these sayings of mine, and doeth them, I will liken him unto a wise man, which built his house upon a rock: [25] And the rain descended, and the floods came, and the winds blew, and beat upon that house; and it fell not: for it was founded upon a rock. [26] And every one that heareth these sayings of mine, and doeth them not, shall be likened unto a foolish man, which built his house upon the sand: [27] And the rain descended, and the floods came, and the winds blew, and beat upon that house; and it fell: and great was the fall of it.

Micah 6:8 He hath shewed thee, O man, what is good; and what doth the Lord require of thee, but to do justly, and to love mercy, and to walk humbly with thy God?
Sometimes I hear people question what is it that God requires of them. They undertake great quests or establish draconian rules to live by. This passage in Deuteronomy simplifies God's requirements. Fear God. Do justice. Love mercy.

Living out this scripture can help make one's walk more complete before God. Just as **2 Peter 1:8** espouses steps to undertake that will ensure fruitful growth in the knowledge of Christ, so too does this passage espouse walking in a way that pleases the Lord.

It seems that in recent years, particularly in geopolitical circles, many have been moved more by rhetoric than character. Others take great pains to make sure their rhetoric emphasizes their values and highlights their character.

Philippians 2:12-13 Wherefore, my beloved, as ye have always obeyed, not as in my presence only, but now much more in my absence, work out your own salvation with fear and trembling. [13] For it is God which worketh in you both to will and to do of his good pleasure.

James 1:22-25 But be ye doers of the word, and not hearers only, deceiving your own selves. [23] For if any be a hearer of the word, and not a doer, he is like unto a man beholding his natural face in a glass: [24] For he beholdeth himself, and goeth his way, and straightway forgetteth what manner of man he was. [25] But whoso looketh into the perfect law of liberty, and continueth therein, he being not a forgetful hearer, but a doer of the work, this man shall be blessed in his deed.

Hebrews 11:5 By faith Enoch was translated that he should not see death; and was not found, because God had translated him: for before his translation he had this testimony, that he pleased God.

We perfect our walk by actually living with an intent to please God in how we live our life. Don't just live to be healthy, wealthy and wise. Live to please the Lord and He will bless you with everything you need. Unfortunately, too many walk in ways that are contrary to pleasing the Lord.

You can perfect your walk. In other words, you can grow in maturity regarding your walk, or how you live by being intentional in living to please God.

Chapter Twelve
PERFECT YOUR SUFFERING
Triumph through Trouble

The Bible is filled with examples of people who suffered trials, tribulations, sickness, loss and death. I am glad that the Bible does not gloss over the diversity of human experience but rather gives a realistic representation of the existence of turmoil and suffering in life. In this chapter I intend to show how we can look at biblical examples, and through them learn how to triumph through our own trials. We can begin with a discussion on general loss and then go on to specific losses; namely health and life.

We all experience loss; be it a favorite item, a cherished heirloom, the loss of status or position; or more tragically the loss of an individual.

Job 1:20-21 Then Job arose, and rent his mantle, and shaved his head, and fell down upon the ground, and worshipped, [21] And said, Naked came I out of my mother's womb, and naked shall I return thither: the Lord gave, and the Lord hath taken away; blessed be the name of the Lord.

Job was a just and upright man. Yet he suffered great personal loss. There is a phrase, recorded three times in the King James Version which highlights the magnitude of Job's suffering. "While he was yet speaking". Think back to a time when it seemed you were continually assailed by attacks and misfortune. That feeling when you couldn't catch a break. If it wasn't one thing, it was another. It seemed like the punches kept coming. Think about that and magnify it.

Job 2:8-10 And he took him a potsherd to scrape himself withal; and he sat down among the ashes. [9] Then said his wife unto him, Dost thou still retain thine integrity? curse God, and die. [10] But he said unto her, Thou speakest as one of the foolish women speaketh. What? shall we receive good at the hand of God, and shall we not receive evil? In all this did not Job sin with his lips.

Thank God for the record of Job's life. It leaves us an example of how God can be with us in the midst of the most intense, varied personal suffering we can endure. Not as the author of our suffering but as the governor or limit on our suffering, and ultimately the savior to deliver us. So great was Job's suffering that his wife asked him to curse God and die. It's probable that this was not malicious. Rather it was out of a sense of concern. She could no longer witness his suffering and wanted his agony to end. The righteous are not exempt from suffering. However, when we invite the Lord into our suffering, He does several things. First, He puts a limit on the suffering which we endure. He commands the evil one on how far our adversary can go. He puts no more on us than we can bear. Often that doesn't appear to be true in the moment. It's only after we have endured through the night to see the figurative morning light, that we understand that we have overcome. I believe past trials are part of our preparation for the trials of today and tomorrow. Consider King David, prior to his ascension to the throne, defeated Goliath. By his own testimony, before he faced Goliath; God had already given him victory over a lion and a bear. As I choose David as an example here, you might not identify with his trial. However you might be able to learn about experience, and how God takes us from victory to victory.

Try this exercise. This exercise is only beneficial if you can see the victories and not just the setbacks. This is not meant to stir up old wounds. So, if you are not yet in that place, build yourself up in your most holy faith and then undertake this exercise. Think back to when you were young and experienced the worst possible thing. Then think about overcoming that. Then progress to the next tragic thing you endured. Remember how you got through that, and so on and so on.

Job was willing to receive both good and evil from the Lord. Job, like many others, probably of God as the original source. An ideology which identifies God as the original source might also think of Him as the cause of everything. I mention this because some blame God for their suffering. Although God uses it all, He is not the author of Job's suffering. Satan is the author. God is the one who puts limits on Satan and does not allow him to press Job beyond what he is able to bear. Also, when God first allows Satan to try Job, its not for Job's destruction but for his proving. There is a passage where David is about to go before Goliath and King Saul wants to give him his armor. David's response was he could not use Saul's armor because he had never tried and proven his armor. At the end of his trial, Job pronounced that he had heard of God, but through his experience he was able to see God. This said something about the experiential knowledge of God. Sometimes the assurance of God's care and power is not realized on the mountain top but in the valley. Not only did Job experience a deeper knowledge of God through his suffering, but the end of Job's trials was that God blessed him with double of all that he lost in his trials. Take these lessons and understanding from Job's example. Uphold your integrity. Don't turn from God. Believe in Him. Trust that God will not allow you to be tempted above what you are able to bear. Look for a deeper relationship with Him and expect that He will reward you.

1 Peter 5:8-10 Be sober, be vigilant; because your adversary the devil, as a roaring lion, walketh about, seeking whom he may devour: [9] Whom resist stedfast in the faith, knowing that the same afflictions are accomplished in your brethren that are in the world. [10] But the God of all grace, who hath called us unto his eternal glory by

***Christ Jesus, after that ye have suffered a while, make you
perfect, stablish, strengthen, settle you.***

Suffering is a part of life- it's inescapable. The only question
is what do you do with the suffering? Do you invite Jesus into
your suffering and let that union strengthen and settle you, or
do you succumb to the suffering, void of hope and let it become
your demise?

***Philippians 3:8 Yea doubtless, and I count all things
but loss for the excellency of the knowledge of Christ Jesus
my Lord: for whom I have suffered the loss of all things,
and do count them but dung, that I may win Christ,***

Be willing to suffer and lose everything to gain Christ. A good
friend once shared with me, "He is no fool who gives up what
he cannot keep to gain what he cannot lose".

***Philippians 3:10-11 That I may know him, and the
power of his resurrection, and the fellowship of his sufferings, being made conformable unto his death; [11] If
by any means I might attain unto the resurrection of the
dead.***

Our desire is to know Jesus fully in the power of His resurrection. Resurrection only comes after death. Some things have
to die to make room for life. One day, as I was talking to my wife
as she was pruning one of her plants, I noticed she had cut into
the green of one of the branches. When I said, "baby I know
you love me, but you are not paying attention to what you are
doing. You cut too low on that branch. There was some green
in that cut." She laughed at me, really laughed. She responded

"No, it's supposed to be like that. I meant to cut that." All the bells went off and I understood. In John 15:1-2, Jesus tells us that He is the true vine, we are the branches, and the Father prunes the branches so that we can bear much fruit.

There is power in giving life and affirming life in the resurrection of Christ Jesus. Realize the power we have to transcend the sufferings of this life. This does not mean we are exempt from suffering, rather we rise above the suffering. The suffering does not keep us down or end in our demise.

1 Corinthians 15:55-57 O death, where is thy sting? O grave, where is thy victory? [56] The sting of death is sin; and the strength of sin is the law. [57] But thanks be to God, which giveth us the victory through our Lord Jesus Christ.

John 16:33 These things I have spoken unto you, that in me ye might have peace. In the world ye shall have tribulation: but be of good cheer; I have overcome the world.

I, like many others, enjoy basking in the promises of God. Understand that the promises of God include trial and suffering. However, that suffering culminates with an overcoming victory and eternal life. The Apostle Paul testifies and affirms this.

2 Timothy 3:11-12 Persecutions, afflictions, which came unto me at Antioch, at Iconium, at Lystra; what persecutions I endured: but out of them all the Lord delivered me. [12] Yea, and all that will live godly in Christ Jesus shall suffer persecution.

Psalm 34:17-19 The righteous cry, and the Lord heareth, and delivereth them out of all their troubles. [18] The Lord is nigh unto them that are of a broken heart; and saveth such as be of a contrite spirit. [19] Many are the afflictions of the righteous: but the Lord delivereth him out of them all.

Although the normal Christian life is filled with suffering, it is not defined by suffering. Rather, it is encompassed with deliverance because the Lord delivers from all our afflictions.

Let us consider a couple of biblical examples.

Daniel 3:15-19 Now if ye be ready that at what time ye hear the sound of the cornet, flute, harp, sackbut, psaltery, and dulcimer, and all kinds of musick, ye fall down and worship the image which I have made; well : but if ye worship not, ye shall be cast the same hour into the midst of a burning fiery furnace; and who is that God that shall deliver you out of my hands? [16] Shadrach, Meshach, and Abed-nego, answered and said to the king, O Nebuchadnezzar, we are not careful to answer thee in this matter. [17] If it be so, our God whom we serve is able to deliver us from the burning fiery furnace, and he will deliver us out of thine hand, O king. [18] But if not, be it known unto thee, O king, that we will not serve thy gods, nor worship the golden image which thou hast set up. [19] Then was Nebuchadnezzar full of fury, and the form of his visage was changed against Shadrach, Meshach, and Abed-nego: therefore he spake, and commanded that they should heat the furnace one seven times more than it was wont to be heated.

1 Corinthians 15:54-57 So when this corruptible shall have put on incorruption, and this mortal shall have put on immortality, then shall be brought to pass the saying that is written, Death is swallowed up in victory. [55] O death, where is thy sting? O grave, where is thy victory? [56] The sting of death is sin; and the strength of sin is the law. [57] But thanks be to God, which giveth us the victory through our Lord Jesus Christ.

In conclusion, don't view suffering as some strange thing. Treat it as part of a Christian's normal journey. Invite the Lord into your suffering. Expect that the Lord will use the experience to deepen your fellowship with Him. Look for His deliverance and reward. One thing that is accomplished in our suffering as it is witnessed by others, is that they get to witness our stand and the power of our mighty God at work in us.

Chapter Thirteen
CONCLUSION

1 Corinthians 1:29-31 That no flesh should glory in his presence. [30] But of him are ye in Christ Jesus, who of God is made unto us wisdom, and righteousness, and sanctification, and redemption: [31] That, according as it is written, He that glorieth, let him glory in the Lord.

The topics we've discussed effect different aspects of our lives. Each one is important because they drive how we live our lives, embark on our journey, and interact in our relationships. Where we stand on each of the topics discussed is reflected in our testimony. Our testimony shows who we are and what we truly believe.

2 Peter 1:2-4 Grace and peace be multiplied unto you through the knowledge of God, and of Jesus our Lord, [3] According as his divine power hath given unto us all things that pertain unto life and godliness, through the knowledge of him that hath called us to glory and virtue: [4] Whereby are given unto us exceeding great and precious promises: that by these ye might be partakers of the divine nature, having escaped the corruption that is in the world through lust.

Ephesians 5:26-27 That he might sanctify and cleanse it with the washing of water by the word, [27] That he might present it to himself a glorious church, not having spot, or wrinkle, or any such thing; but that it should be holy and without blemish.

People often compartmentalize their lives, to the degree that they are one person in their church life, another in their work environment, and yet someone else in their family life. The Lord wants to make us whole, complete and free of defects in Him. There is no condemnation in Christ Jesus.

In the quest for perfection, these individual aspects are often isolated and treated as if one can excel in any one of the chapter headings and reach perfection. Perfection or wholeness is in our relationship to the Godhead which created, redeems and sustains. So, to be perfect would be to learn to invite the Lord into every aspect of life and let Him bring fullness, wholeness, healing and completeness to your life. In Him is everything we need.

Philippians 3:14-15 I press toward the mark for the prize of the high calling of God in Christ Jesus. [15] Let us therefore, as many as be perfect, be thus minded: and if in any thing ye be otherwise minded, God shall reveal even this unto you.